DEATH &
DIVINITY...

DEATH &
DIVINITY...

HOW SWEET IT IS...

Judith Gamble

BALBOA.
PRESS
A DIVISION OF HAY HOUSE

Balboa Press books may be ordered through booksellers or by contacting:

Balboa Press
A Division of Hay House
1663 Liberty Drive
Bloomington, IN 47403
www.balboapress.com
1-(877) 407-4847

Because of the dynamic nature of the Internet, any web addresses or links contained in this book may have changed since publication and may no longer be valid. The views expressed in this work are solely those of the author and do not necessarily reflect the views of the publisher, and the publisher hereby disclaims any responsibility for them.

The author of this book does not dispense medical advice or prescribe the use of any technique as a form of treatment for physical, emotional, or medical problems without the advice of a physician, either directly or indirectly. The intent of the author is only to offer information of a general nature to help you in your quest for emotional and spiritual well-being. In the event you use any of the information in this book for yourself, which is your constitutional right, the author and the publisher assume no responsibility for your actions.

Any people depicted in stock imagery provided by Thinkstock are models, and such images are being used for illustrative purposes only.

Certain stock imagery © Thinkstock.

ISBN: 978-1-4525-3839-6 (e)
ISBN: 978-1-4525-3840-2 (sc)

Printed in the United States of America

Balboa Press rev. date: 11/21/2011

about the title . . . *I chose the word Death* . . .

Then I awaited help from "the invisible forces" for the remainder . . .

Divinity . . . ***how sweet it is*** . . . *quickly appeared. I knew this was from my sweet mother.*

While living she had written several books as a "Ghostwriter" . . .

Along with her great sense of humor she loved double meanings . . .

She was letting me know how sweet Death is . . .

Divinity, refers to "The essence of God" as well as my" favorite childhood candy"!

Mom and I would happily spend Saturday mornings together . . . *cooking and tasting,* **Divinity** . . . ***how sweet it was !***

CONTENTS

DEDICATION

For Dr. Elisabeth Kubler-Ross . . . who taught the world of Death and Dying . . .
She knew that Death does not really exist and devoted her life to prove it . . .
She taught me not to fear Death . . .

For Jean Weber-Lomax . . . The Best Mom ever . . . my Mentor
Who guided this free-spirit giving me the greatest gifts of all . . .
Life and the Freedom to follow my own path . . .

For Kimo . . . my Son . . . an Angel . . .
Who taught so many . . . including myself . . .
Compassion and Love . . .

For my blue-eyed Friend . . .
I learned that Unconditional Love is forever . . .

I LOVE YOU ALL . . .
This lifetime . . .
Past lifetimes . . .
and Future lifetimes we shall share . . .

FOREWORD

It is a rare gift when we can look into the heart and life of someone who has faced death and loss and come out stronger and wiser.

I was blessed to know Judy at a weeklong workshop on Maui with Elisabeth Kubler-Ross M.D. many years ago. That week changed my life forever and set me down a path of Spiritual Realization and service.

Judy's presence along with her little son, Kimo, opened a door and helped me down a path that has given my life meaning and value beyond anything I could have imagined.

Death and Divinity shares with us a personal journey of a mother struggling to accept the untimely death of her little son. Like so many of us, she is filled with fear and desperately tries to hold on to his fragile life. Her journey for understanding, support and acceptance unfold in mysterious ways. We are fortunate to have someone like Judy, with a gift to clearly share her personal journey and the wisdom, gained along the way.

Too many of us are afraid to look death squarely in the face and discover that it is an illusion: We are born of Spirit and live in that eternal reality. We get caught in the collective delusion that life is only material and that all is lost with the passing of the physical body.

For those who have the courage and God's grace to look deeper, they find that the Soul is real, tangible and eternal. When the inner vision is open we see we have not lost anyone; they merely exist in a more subtle reality. We only need to learn how to see and listen in a different way to keep that contact and feel their love and support as we continue here on earth.

I have had both parents and a younger brother pass on. I was with my father and at his passing the room became filled with a golden light and a very sublime presence that was almost breathless. His love and presence was tangible. I spent three hours in that sacred space. Sometimes I see him now; feeling his watchful presence. It is a comfort to know that we are still connected.

So many are devastated when someone they love dies. The emptiness and pain are too much to bear. I know from my own clinical experience that death looses its terrible sting when our eyes and heart are open to see more.

Life, here, seems so real that we forget we are living in a dream within a dream.

When we pass on and wake up, we have a bigger vision and a greater understanding about our earthly life and role. The more we can make friends with death and realize that it is only a dream, we will be more empowered to live our life with wisdom, courage, purpose and direction.

Judy, like me, received help, love and wisdom from Elisabeth Kubler-Ross M.D. We were blessed to know her and our lives were forever changed

Death & Divinity is a tribute to Judy's courage and part of the legacy from Elisabeth. This is a book worth reading because of it's authenticity, clarity and depth of wisdom.

Ronald L. Mann, Ph.D.

INTRODUCTION

Death does not exist . . . *how sweet is that?*

What does exist is *"The fear of Death"*! I bring proof of this through my own experiences, even to my more skeptic readers, for I was once, the most skeptic of all.

Death & Divinity . . . *how sweet it is* . . . is a blend of my own life experiences, research and those of my teachers, sprinkled with sweetness from the invisible forces . . . Divinity!

I first invite readers to journey with me down my own path beginning with the most profound week of my life! I had been searching with all my heart, to find the truth of life after death. My son, Kimo had spent his entire first year in Intensive Care and after all the ups and downs, dying five times, and when all hope was gone he was sent home to die.

I was thankful for every moment that he lived but at the same time I felt as if I were on a yo-yo ride. I loved his up times, heartbroken on the down, but mostly I was suspended in mid air, never knowing from one day to the next when his last day would be. His tank of oxygen was my best friend but after three years on this continuous ride I could take no more. I had many questions that I needed answers to. I needed my mind and heart to be set at peace in order to deal with the inevitable . . . his death.

My many one-on-one's with God finally paid off in what seemed a coincidence. I was invited to attend a week's workshop led by Dr. Elisabeth Kubler-Ross, who was the utmost authority of the day and had written her international ground breaking book, *On Death and Dying*. She would certainly have all the answers for me.

I believed her workshop to be strictly academic in nature and was completely unaware of the incredible forces surrounding this great lady. I was also unaware that this would be the most profound week of my life!

It was at Elisabeth's workshop that I met Ronald Mann, Ph.D. who was a young psychologist from Beverly Hills. He experienced a "spontaneous spiritual awakening" during this amazing week. Following the workshop he went on to integrate spirituality with his psychotherapy and wrote his Bestseller *Sacred Healing*, a dynamic validation of his healing through Mind, Body and Spirit.

I had no idea what an out of body experience was until the last evening of Elisabeth's workshop when I became swept up in the energy of what I call the "Cosmic Sea". I suddenly found myself looking down and seeing my physical body. Somehow my Soul had tapped into a small fragment of our Universal Consciousness.

It was during this mind shifting experience that I was given all the answers to my many questions about death. It was also at this moment of realization that I lost all fear of death . . . at the same time I became aware how we are ALL connected through this energy field. Our Souls remaining separate; but still connected to the core. To this day I still find it difficult in describing this invisible field of reality which had become so visible and interactive.

Stepping ahead, Gregg Braden explains quite clearly in *Divine Matrix*, leaving no questionable doubt of our connectivity with the Universe. He's internationally known as a pioneer in bridging science and spirituality.

Stepping back again . . . unfinished business was part of Elisabeth's agenda so immediately following her workshop, upon my return to Honolulu; I honored her, my son, myself and God by getting rid of the oxygen tank. I now trusted in God. It was several years later that my son passed away, then I moved to Maui. Lots of sprinkles from Divinity came my way but I wasn't able to relate to anyone regarding my new found awareness. Later I left the Islands, taking refuge in Corporate America in Los Angeles . . . leaving paradise for the city of Angels.

My Corporate path came to a halt with the California Recession. It was at a time when I wasn't ready to expose my true self. My ego still cared what people might think, but further along on my journey, I ended up doing what I should have been doing all the while . . . pursuing my spiritual quest so that I could help others some day.

A friend gave me Louise Hay's book, *You Can Heal Your Life*. I was back on track . . . and blessed to have met her at the 2007 I Can Do It Conference in Las Vegas. A whole new chain of coincidences was beginning, or let me call them sprinkles from divinity. I was crossing the street, headed for the convention center: there lay a dead pedestrian in the middle of the crosswalk. I missed the sign and it's meaning at the time, but, definitely got the message later on.

I can't say enough about Dr. Wayne W. Dyer and how much he has inspired me to go forward when life seemed anything but fair. It's all here in chapter eight: let me say, he ignites any room where he makes an appearance, and you will get caught up in his positive energy and his most powerful messages!

Being a free spirit I've taken chances out-of-the-box so as to increase my Soul awareness and expand my horizons, as they say. At one point it just made sense to attend a past life regression workshop which was led by the creditable and utmost authority, Dr. Brian Weiss, graduate of Columbia, Yale School of Medicine and bestselling author of *Many lives Many Masters*.

My intention was to attend his workshop only as an observer, not as a participant. I ended up having an incredible past life regression myself. This experience connected many missing pieces to my present lifetime and continues on to make sense of life.

I had to have another regression because the first was so enlightening and once again with Dr. Weiss. During my regressions I met up with my blue-eyed friend from this life time, finding him in three previous lives. Oh yes, Elisabeth showed up during my first regression which supports further proof of synchronicity, adding further support to human connectedness, as you shall see.

Past life regressions have also validated my own beliefs in reincarnation, something proven to me over thirty years ago. Mark Twain embraced reincarnation, and he writes in his autobiography "I have been born more times than anybody except Krishna." He also saw the connection in coincidence . . . "I came in with Halley's comet . . . I expect to go out with it", which he did, having been born the same year the comet came and died the same year the comet left.

We sometimes can't explain why or even make a connection at the time an insignificant event occurs, but everything does happen for a reason, believe it or not! Chapter Ten is a perfect example showing how an ordinary day, an ordinary trip to a book store turns into a really significant bit of synchronicity for me. Everything came full circle beginning with just one deed, overlooked as a message materializing from that other side, the invisible God side. What's amazing is that none of it would have happened to me if Carolyn Myss, New York Times bestselling Author, had not written *Sacred Contracts*.

As I journeyed along my path I couldn't help but marvel at the abundance of joy along the way. I'm thankful for all the curves, the peaks and valleys that have been there . . . and all the rest, the sunsets, oceans, roses . . . I've always stopped to smell the roses . . .

As I leave memory lane I see it's time to look forward to the future . . . but first one last glance at the past, a chapter I called Time Prompt 11:11 which is laced with some pretty unbelievable elevener signs . . . some coming from half way round the world . . . others beyond.

My last Chapter is all about the future 12-21-2012 . . .

We are all headed in that direction and It really doesn't matter which path you are on right now. There are no detours around 12-21-2012. I am keeping my positive mindset throughout the looming media storms drawing momentum as we get closer to the date of the end . . . the end of the Mayan calendar.

The dooms day people believe the world comes to an end December 21, 2012. The Bible people believe that the world's coming to an end but they don't agree on the date . . . Me, I believe as Gregg Braden in *Fractal Time*, that it's the end of time as we know it . . . not the end of the World!

Gregg suggests that "We have the power we need to create all the changes we choose". We're not just observers, we are the creators and we are all connected . . . he gives a formula to determine the number of people needed to work together to bring about world peace. The figures are very achievable and we can make it happen . . .

Barbara Marx Hubbard, one of modern day's greatest visionaries is brought to light in *The Mother of Invention* by Neale Donald Walsch. She has a plan for "Day One" which is December 22, 2012. How much more positive can you get than that? I like her plan and you can be a part of it too. This is her gift to all of us.

Death & Divinity . . . *how sweet it is* . . . is my gift to you. It's a gift that is meant to bring peace of mind and hope when you are faced with the loss of a friend, family member or yourself, whether it be past, present or in the future. Sprinkles from Divinity are within reach, just waiting for you to reach out and connect with them.

Until we meet . . . again, again and again . . .

CHAPTER ONE

Most Profound Week

Excerpt from *Sacred Healing:* Author: Ronald Mann, Ph.D.
Regarding the Elisabeth Kubler-Ross M.D. workshop, Maui, Hawaii

"I was some what taken aback at the levels of human suffering and pain that were being shared. Many had children who had just died or parents who were in the process of dying. One woman had even brought her 3-year-old child who had multiple birth defects and was kept alive through intravenous feedings. His health was so poor that she carried oxygen with her, because he had difficulty breathing on his own. We were all aware that this little boy could die at any time, and we wondered if this was the place he would choose to leave his body"

I was this woman with her dying 3-year-old child . . .
Dr Mann was correct . . . my little boy could die at any time . . .
However, he chose another time and place to leave his body . . .

Excerpts from letter written to me by Elisabeth:
Author *On Death and Dying*

"My dear, dear Judy

Thank you for sharing and letting me know that our very special, beloved Kimo is now in this Super-Special and Beautiful place where we all end up one day when we have finished our tasks and able and permitted to graduate . . . I guess you will always know how much I treasure the time we had together with Kimo and with you on that special Island . . . I am leaving soon for the east coast, then 4 countries in Europe but did not want to take off without writing you at least a little letter to tell you I love you and rejoice with you that Kimo can now dance, talk, laugh and sing again and he will naturally continue to help us in our earthly struggles to make this place a little more compassionate and loving . . . some things he taught so many people during his short earth-stay".

"Be well and happy in your new environment, I love Maui and you . . . Elisabeth"

Most Profound Week

My Son was born to die . . . therefore began the creation of the most profound week of my life!

Traditionally a book starts at the beginning. My life hadn't been traditional, with that being said, it just makes good sense that I should begin during the most significant week of my entire life.

Off to the beautiful Island of Maui I headed with pen in hand . . . my dying son in one arm and his oxygen tank in the other . . . to attend Dr. Elisabeth Kubler-Ross's death and dying workshop.

Believing the coming week was to be strictly academic in nature my intention was to get to the truth of life after death from the utmost authority of the day! She was well known internationally by the medical field for openly addressing death with patients and their families.

I was totally unaware of the week that lay ahead in which I would experience some pretty far-out things, things that I had only heard of and some that I hadn't heard of. I would became a believer in Reincarnation and I would soon learn that nothing happens by coincidence, that everything happens for a reason, although we may not see it that way at the time.

My son had died clinically multiple times, spending more than a year in intensive care then sent home to die, in my care, a thought I couldn't bare. Now was the perfect time for this "Angel of Mercy" from Heaven and Switzerland to come into my life. I thought it odd to be living my childhood dream of moving to Hawaii and living in paradise but somehow I had gotten caught up living life in my own mental hell, which would change by the end of the week.

My husband was too busy to attend and probably a bit too cowardly to attend . . . just as I might have been had I known ahead about the coming week, particularly that last evening. This would become the moment of truth, when I would loose my *Fear of Death* forever. My mind would soon be blown away!

I had met Elisabeth as we were boarding the plane in Honolulu, arriving late at the airport which was part of my soon to be ex-husband's plan. He had wanted me to miss the flight and the workshop from the very start. Elisabeth had managed to have the plane delayed until Kimo and I were on board! This indicated to me the power of this great lady and proved to me that I was truly in the right place, at the right time . . . just running a bit late.

I loved these short scenic flights to the outer Islands with the awesome turquoise water along the shoreline changing to deeper tones of blue the further out we flew and then changing into white surf pounding the tropical beach as we got closer. Haleakala Crater was always spectacular rising over 10,000 feet in the air.

My thoughts turned to my husband as I remembered my first flight to Maui, which was with him . . . how I wished things could have been different but too much had happened between us and his best friend Mr. Bottle.

We were approaching for landing at the Kahului airport which was unique at the time, comprised of a huge dome with the circular top cut away allowing plenty of room for the massive Banyan tree growing beneath. We disembarked, climbed aboard the van and soon we would be headed upcountry towards the gigantic slopes of Haleakala, known as a very spiritual place.

Upon arrival at the retreat I found myself surrounded with what seemed somewhat of a "Huggy" group". Something which I wasn't used to nor was I prepared for . . . having not hugged or been hugged much in my life, I was somewhat uncomfortable in this environment! I definitely was not in my comfort zone and this certainly did not appear to be the academic group I had imagined.

I was out of my realm but I was on the most important mission of my life so I decided to just "get over it" keep my mind open and follow my heart. I had come too far now to turn back and guess what? By the end of that week it was easy for me to hug and be hugged, and not only that, but those hugs felt pretty damn good!

I don't remember his name but I surely remember his hug filled with deep compassion on our last day of the workshop. He apologized to me adding that he had been upset with me for bringing a child to this type of retreat but now he was thanking me profusely because it had meant so much to him. His words truly touched my heart, as my son had touched his heart, not only a little more compassionate but I believe he had learned another lesson from Elisabeth on the subject of not being judgmental . . . something which I learned! Wasn't it I whom had judged the group as too "huggy"?

Ghostly Eyes

Dr. Ron Mann was a child psychologist from Beverly Hills who worked with children. I felt a special bond with him as I knew that he was working with a little three year old boy with a brain tumor. As it turned out, this child became one of his greatest teachers in life.

The first day I saw Dr. Ron he had a really glazed look in his eyes which I can only explain that I felt as if "he had seen a ghost" and in a sense he had. I felt that though he was looking directly at me he wasn't seeing me. This blank stare was of endless depth and I now know that I was seeing his Soul. They say that our eyes are windows to the soul and I truly believe this.

I learned that he had experienced something spiritual that first day. I was unaware of this at the time but he had regressed to a past life and was experiencing life during the Holocaust which he later wrote about. He had a sudden realization that he was a child walking through a hallway of showers, the gas chamber in Nazi Germany where at the far end of the showers he had seen a pile of bodies stacked and in decay.

Years later I was on the internet looking for information about Elisabeth's workshop on Maui when I ran across Dr. Ron. I emailed and got in touch with him when he mentioned his book "Sacred Healing". I was humbled and honored by the fact that he wrote about me and my son in his book and that, that week turned out to be the most important week of his life!

He writes that he discovered after speaking with Elisabeth that they had both been together at the time of Christ and had been looking for one another for a long, long time. While engaging in energy balancing, becoming more connected to the human emotions, he realized the oneness of the universe, seeing all human interconnectedness. This is something we all share, but it's from a different energy field.

I find it quite fascinating that while we both had come from very different walks of life, we had both ended up in the middle of the Pacific Ocean, on this small island to address the same issue . . . *our own personal fear of death*!

Elisabeth not only proved to myself that there is no death, but that there are no coincidences, that everything happens for a reason . . . everything!

One early morning Elisabeth, Ron and some of the others piled into a van and headed up the dark slopes of Haleakala Crater for Sunrise. This is always a *next to GOD* experience to observe crystal clear stars, surrounded by crispy fresh air, total darkness and absolute silence all at the same time.

This morning the air was filled with a burst of Sandalwood fragrance except there was no incense and it would be next to impossible for it to burn at 10,000 feet, where it is next to freezing.

Amazingly everyone in the van had heard a choir of spirits singing in high soprano on the way up to the summit.

Then it was time for God's spectacular painting of every imaginable color and design as the sun began to rise and darkness disappeared with the advent of crimson reds, oranges and yellows all giving way to purple hues turning into an awesome beautiful blue sky.

Elisabeth

It was before the group's trip to the summit of Haleakala that I too, had smelled the essence similar to the fragrance of sandalwood. It was in the alcove just off the main meeting room where Elisabeth would meet with some of us at the close of day. Elisabeth assured us that this was an essence from her "spirit guides" letting her know that they were around her.

I had no idea what a spirit guide was until that week and being a bit skeptical I searched for incense, ashes, matches and smoke, but found nothing that indicated anyone could be burning incense. According to all that is scientific and physical the essence was impossible, but still it was there, only when Elisabeth was there.

My days ended with that wonderful smell of incense under the Alcove where we would finish up the day by singing "You Are My Sunshine" in honor of her guides. Her main guide had been a tall Native American named Salem. As a child Elisabeth had been drawn to Indian symbols, having danced on a flat rock in warrior style without ever being exposed to that culture. The night before arriving to live in the United States with her new groom she dreamed of herself dressed as an Indian riding horseback across the desert.

My mornings began with dear Elisabeth presenting my son with a little fresh flower from the outside garden. His face would light up in the biggest grin, which lit up my heart. Not only could you feel her love, you could see it, she spoke of love and unconditional love.

She viewed death as simply shedding of the physical body like the butterfly sheds its cocoon. She had witnessed messages and pictures of butterflies drawn by children on the walls of the German concentration camps. These butterflies were left by the children before they would enter the gas chambers. Elisabeth showed us modern day pictures drawn by children who were her dying patients and pointed out how she could tell that they knew they were dying without ever being told.

Workshop continues

Elisabeth asked me on several occasions when I would be sharing my story with the group but I wasn't sure I could at that point. Some things were still too close to my own heart and I had never addressed my sadness and fears in front of a group before. I wasn't sure I could keep my composure long enough for it all to make sense to the others.

Our group consisted of doctors, nurses, clergy, professors and family members who had lost or were loosing loved ones. A grieving mother who's son had died in my son's hospital room was there. She had aged considerably but by the end of Elisabeth's magical week she appeared ten or fifteen years younger, her face radiant, I sensed she was really at peace.

I had remembered the day they flew her child by emergency air from the island of Kauai after almost drowning. I also remembered seeing him as he lay in critical condition not far from my son's incubator. I felt saddened the day when I arrived at the hospital and his little bed was empty. I almost felt guilty and at the same time very fortunate that I still had my son, all though she had lost hers.

There were several in the group who were going to scatter ashes of loved ones. Elisabeth spoke to them and described how human ashes appeared after cremation, which would be different than the finer ashes, that they might be expecting to see.

Elisabeth explained the five stages of death, the denial, the anger, bargaining, depression and acceptance. When Elisabeth spoke you listened, her voice was entirely unique with an angelic quality, her delightful Swiss accent and of course her subject matter was distinct and one of interest to everyone in the room. She was known for her first book *On Death and Dying* in which she first introduced the five stages to the world.

I had made it through the denial stage by facing his death everyday for three years. I had made it through anger most the time simply because I felt so fortunate every day that he lived. I wasn't sure how God's goodness worked, at that point. This angered me off and on but then I would remind myself of the bargain I had struck up with God. It went something like this "if you let me keep Kimo for five and a half years so that I may lavish him with love, then I shall give him back for you to keep".

I was stuck and had been stuck for some time ... not able to accept his inevitable death! I had been given hope and encouragement so many times.

My time to share

Kimo was happily swaying in his "Jolly Jumper" which was a swing attached to the top of the doorway between the main meeting room and kitchen area. I introduced him and said that he was dying . . . then through the tears, how much I loved him and through more tears I managed to convey that I didn't think I could handle his final death although he had died before.

A female voice shouted across the room, Why don't you just let him die?" Her words pierced my aching heart and shocked me! At that point a nun stood and firmly stated to that female . . . "Damn you . . . how dare you judge her" . . . then Elisabeth broke in and reminded the group about the importance of being non-judgmental.

I wasn't aware until that moment that Nun's ever swore, but It made me feel damn good that a member of the clergy and a world re-known Doctor, both had come to my support. Up until that moment I had thought I was a really good mother, in other words, I was doing the best I could. It had never crossed my mind to let him die. This was what Elisabeth was all about . . . the fact that the Medical professionals did not discuss this taboo subject with patients.

I later learned that this awesome Nun who had voiced her opinion had taken a temporary leave from the church to sort out some personal issues. I only know that in that one week most of us learned much of life, unconditional love, coincidence and death. We had moved beyond our early conditionings, society's ideas expectations and values.

Mind Over Matter

One of the participants attending the workshop was an American-Japanese Professor, born and raised in Hawaii. He clearly was well versed in Martial arts, had practiced mind control and began his centering demonstration commanding silence from the group. He then focused on surrounding himself with a pure white light of protection, which we were unable to see the light, but clearly the energy was there.

He then invited volunteers to try to touch, push or shove him. Not one person could break through this invisible protective light. Three or four of the group, different weights, physical sizes and strengths tried to strike him but could not break through this amazing force. His demonstration was proof to me that we, as human beings, live in multi faceted dimensions of energy. The light energy goes unseen due to the density of vibrations but because we are programmed to believe that if you can't see it, then it's not real. This was very real . . .

Powerful Connection

Hawaiians have a powerful connection to the ocean, their land and believing there are places where spirits of their ancestors continue to watch over the land and it's people. I had seen several ghosts in Hawaii but several objects manifested this week which had to do with legends from the ancients. I had not previously heard or read about them but now they would appear.

One night Elisabeth had the group step outside to view the "night rainbow". It seemed very close to the retreat, stretching out towards the ocean. It was the perfect shape of a massive rainbow except that it had no vibrant colors, only that of a deep white mist. Years later I learned that this is a very spiritual sign of protection from the ancestors and that not many are fortunate to be graced with its appearance. Living in Hawaii for seventeen years I had never once seen the night rainbow before that evening, or did I see it afterward.

Legend has it that if you are fortunate to view the Sacred Owl, it will bring good fortune your way. Some of us, including Elisabeth, took the van in hopes of spotting this infamous pueo. We headed down a dark road lined with trees, where in the headlights appeared the white feathers of this notorious bird sitting in a tree just staring at us. He was within close viewing distance of the road, which he's most known to do on moonlit nights.

They say Pueo watches out for someone close to the dying. Once again, just like the night of the rainbow I never saw the "protector or Sacred Owl" again. It was only in this most profound week that I saw both . . . both in Elisabeth's presence. She had the energy to bring fourth her Spirit guides, so was it possible that she was able to bring fourth energy from the ancestors?

Last Evening . . . New Awareness

It was the last evening of the workshop. I felt more comfortable about death and knew that there would be life after death for my son. I knew that I would manage to get through it all somehow. It would be the deep missing of his presence that I would have to deal with, which I missed him even now, just knowing that he would be gone. I felt blessed, but torn . . . If there were only something visual that I could see: some actual material evidence of life after death.

I was sitting on the floor talking to Auntie Anne, one of my son's favorite ICU nurses. My guess was that Anne had attended the workshop partly because of me and Kimo, and also for herself. She had gotten me interested in Astrology as she was very knowledgeable on the subject. She had always referred to herself as a very old soul and I had no idea how she could possibly have known, but she did.

Elisabeth very graciously, was making the rounds with each and every attendee expressing words of encouragement, thanking all of us for attending and bidding us all a fond farewell with a loving hug.

She asked me if her work shop had helped and then asked if I were interested in coming to her healing center, being developed outside of San Diego, California, called Shanti Nilaya. This was a place for the dying and their families. Her invitation was very endearing and took me by complete surprise. I told her that I wouldn't know until later . . . later became now!

What's Up Now

The exact moment Elisabeth left my view I could feel the energy change around me. It took me years before I could tell anyone about what happened next. My ego would not allow me to tell, in fear that everyone would think I was crazy. It didn't seem possible, but yet, it is as vivid in my mind today as it was then.

I was still sitting on the floor, speaking with Auntie Anne who sat on the end of the couch next to me. I was also looking across the room at my son, content in his swing, when an extraordinary beam of bright, white light suddenly appeared high above him. The light entered much like a falling star descends across the sky, coming closer and becoming larger.

At closer view this mass of bright light was filled with what appeared to be 3-Dimensional bubble-like circles, each having a single but prominent and protruding black dot within it. All were moving along in a bouncing wave like motion that ended with a swirling wave.

The only humanly way to describe these circles or bubbles, is that each was similar to the yin and yang symbol but minus the black half. There was only a thin trace of grey dividing the two halves. Unlike the yin and yang there was only one dot which I would soon know to be a soul.

Miraculously, I left my body merging into one of the black dots . . . my own soul! I was having an out of body experience. I was in the midst of an OBE because looking down from within the light I could see my physical body below, still talking to Auntie Anne, but at the same time I was up here. I was in my own continuum reviewing my lives, much like the shuffling of cards at the end of a winning computer solitaire game, where the cards can shuffle forever. I could see all my lives . . . past, present and future, except that there was no beginning and there was no end. I not only knew and saw my own eternity but also that of everyone else at the workshop, and all at the same time.

I felt as if time had no meaning, that I was weightless, sort of floating on water, and that all of us were connected. We were connected at the core, through all of our lives, but at the same time each of us carried with us our one Soul which gave us a separate identity in the Universe.

I knew everyone, every life, every name in every life, every address in every country, every gender, and every reason for being in every life, throughout all of eternity . . . it was like tapping into the akashic records, which for good reason isn't meant for us as humans to remember the details, and I didn't. What I knew was that it is all about Reincarnation. As quickly as it all happened it was all over except I've always remembered that I knew everything and everything made perfect sense . . . and it was all so uncomplicated.

In a split second I was back sitting on the floor speaking to Auntie Anne . . . but there was one more thing . . . as the two of us were ending our conversation her facial features began changing right before my eyes from that of a pretty twenty-eight year old woman into an ancient being. I have never seen someone that old. She looked thousands of years old . . . and then in an instant her face was back to that of twenty-eight years, her wrinkles from thousands of years gone! She had been right all along . . . she was a very old soul.

Lost Fear

Instantly I had lost all fear of death for my son and everyone. I tried to find Elisabeth, to share my experience, and to let her know that I would not need to attend Shanti Nilaya.

Everything happened so quickly, the workshop was over, all of us left the retreat and I was back in Honolulu finishing up some unfinished business which was a portion of Elisabeth's agenda.

In honor of Elisabeth and God, my son and myself I immediately got rid of Kimo's tank of Oxygen. I no longer needed it because I now trusted in God again, and the invisible forces. I now was able to accept my son's death on God's terms . . .

CHAPTER TWO

Spirit Guides-Penguins and Such

I never did tell Anne that I now knew she was a very old soul, maybe thousands of years old, and I had seen her change right before my eyes. It was not a pretty sight and I've often wondered if I may have changed before her eyes, too . . . I'll never know because we lost contact after that.

During the last night of Elisabeth's workshop, as I was speaking with Auntie Anne, we were discussing her upcoming trip to Europe. She asked if I might like to take over her house sitting commitment for two and a half months. If she had asked before the workshop I would have thought this to be just a coincidence but now I knew and understood the significance of what seems a coincidence. I remembered Elisabeth's words, once again, that everything happens for a reason.

I was ecstatic with the opportunity that this would give me a way out of my unhappy home and away from Jim for a couple of months. By now my husband was avoiding home as much as possible. We were growing apart more and more as time went on.

Our only spoken words turned into arguments. I needed to get Kimo away from this type of environment. House sitting seemed the perfect answer to a wish come true, covered with sprinkles from Divinity.

High on the Ridge

It was easy to make the move because Jim really liked Auntie Anne and we were both glad that I could help her out, after all that she had done for Kimo during his hospital stays. My son and I moved high upon the slopes of Wilhelmina Ridge from the slopes of Punchbowl crater. At the time we had no way of knowing that we were living on the slopes of the crater that would become our son's final resting place.

I became somewhat apprehensive just before the move to the ridge because of the rumors I had heard. It seems there were several burglaries on that street. The neighborhood was quite nice and the house was beautiful, with nicely landscaped yards and a gorgeous swimming pool. There were two precious dogs that were part of the house sitting deal, but unfortunately these two were not watch dogs. I decided it was a good move anyway, and so I followed my heart, and I just gave my fears to the forces.

After learning of spirit guides at the work shop I knew I had a couple of my own to protect me. I also knew that coincidence happened for a reason so I didn't think too much about my first night when the dogs and I were in the front yard, a yard light blew out, then again on the second night. The third night I flipped the hallway light switch on, but the light blew out. This was going on almost everyday . . . then I finally figured it out . . . It had to be my spirit guides, Angels or something from the other side. By now I had heard that electricity was a way the spirit realm could contact you . . . and so it was . . .

One evening I had a small group from Elisabeth's workshop up for dinner. After they left I was doing the final clean up and turned the light to the chandelier off but it stayed on. Believe me it was bright. The way the house was situated in the crater this light was brightly shining into many of the neighbor's homes . . . so how were they going to sleep. I tried the switch again but the chandelier wouldn't turn off . . . It was already late so I went and changed to my night-T, came back to the dining room and tried the light once again. I decided to heck with the neighbors they would just have to have a sleepless night!

I went to bed, after lying there a few minutes I decided I couldn't leave the light on, running the risk of a massive light bill for the homeowners, so I got up and gave it one last shot and guess what? The chandelier immediately went out and it struck me like a bolt of lightning . . . this definitely had to be my guides trying to get in touch with me through electricity. They wanted me to know they were protecting me. I never worried about becoming burglarized again.

Another thing that had my concern, just a bit . . . how the heck was I going to replace the light bulbs when the owners of the house returned from vacation. I decided not to worry until the time came. Kimo and I continued relaxing in the wonderful Hawaiian sun and swimming in the pool. It was next to heaven . . . every now and then I would try to turn on the lights that had burned out, but none of them did light up . . .

Time marched on and the owners of the house were due to return within a week. It saddened me to be leaving because we had, had such a good time. By then lights were burned out all over the place in most every room; a lamp in the TV room, a huge lamp in the downstairs living room, a kitchen stove light, a bathroom light, a bedroom lamp, in addition to the original hallway light and six yard lights.

I tried turning them all on again, but, nothing happened. I made my list and decided to go shopping the day before the owners arrived home. The day came and I decided to do one final walk through, just in case . . . and guess what? Every single light came on, in the hall, the living room, bedroom, the stove light and even all the yard lights came back on. This just doesn't happen in our reality. By all odds It would be impossible for all of them to light up again, especially at the exact time I needed them too . . . pure coincidence, I don't think so . . .

I learned to believe more and more in this invisible force as a protective force, one that I had given my fears to when I first heard about the burglaries. I learned that the force is always there for us and I also found that these sprinkles from Divinity try to communicate with us offering their assistance. It's up to us to pick up on the messages.

Another safe place

Sometime during my stay up on the ridge, our condo, on the slopes of Punchbowl had been broken into and almost everything stolen. The Property Manager was a witness to the break-in, and from his description, I knew who was responsible. These three thieves had the manager convinced they were helping us move and because of their reputations I did not want to pursue any legal matters. I was happy enough to have my life and my son's life, for a while longer.

I was so naïve. I never quite understood how anyone could have the heart to take our rocking chair that I rocked Kimo to sleep in. One of the three and his wife had been over for dinner once, so they knew that our son was dying . . . they had watched me as I rocked him to sleep . . . it didn't seem to matter that this chair was one of his few pleasures. Most my clothes were taken but possessions become quite meaningless when it comes to love, life and death.

Several amazing things happened in my favor . . . more sprinkles from the invisible . . . Jim was out of town as usual. I got paid enough for house sitting to move into a downtown condo with live security. My instructions to the guards were not to allow Jim in the building.

I spent time with Kimo on the rooftop gardens while studying for my Real Estate exam. Jim, meantime stayed at the empty condo . . . or so he said.

It had been a while since Elisabeth's workshop so as time went on it was easy to forget the positive, once you become surrounded with negative. I still trusted in God but that trust was diminishing, so I decided to test God . . . in my mind because there was no mail delivery that day, which was a Sunday, it would be impossible, I dared God to bring me a gift that day.

I went about my day, placing my gift from God on the back burner. Kimo and I went to the garden for fun and so that I could study. Later on in the day I decided to go for a walk, and on the way back, we stopped by the grocery store where we ran into Kimo's favorite Auntie Clerk. She ran up and immediately smothered him with kisses then she left and came back in a few minutes.

Penguin Test

She returned with a toy . . . a little windup penguin with little plastic feet that flipped about making this hilarious clicking noise which really got the three of us laughing. Kimo continued his cute giggling, so the more he giggled the more we wound the winder and this went on for a good ten minutes until it was time for Auntie Clerk to get back to work. I realized I had gotten my impossible gift from God which was far better than any gift I had imagined!

What better gift could a parent receive than seeing the joy and laughter of their children? For me this was pure validation that God never left our side. I remembered as a child the sight of Nuns dressed in black and white habits, their dress always reminded me of Penguin's . . . and God!

This new penguin became a favorite toy of Kimo's along with his magic apple, which was his favorite bathtub toy, a huge red plastic apple that bounced around in the water making cute chiming noises that really tickled my son in the tub. It brought me much joy listening to the chiming and giggling. Another favorite toy was his stuffed Tiger which was musical, and had been a favorite of the nurses and doctors, so much so, that the music box wore out. One of the doctors performed a music-box-ectomy on tiger, which brought back the music and also touched me deeply.

Penguins started popping up everywhere: cards, signs and I started a collection . . . they've been following me for years . . . It's so fun when I get one . . . I think of God and the invisible forces sending these messages of encouragement, that I'm not alone, and that I am where I need to be. Shortly after GOD passed his penguin test, he helped me pass my Real Estate test.

I passed my Real Estate exam at an excellent time when the real estate market was on its way up. I knew I'd be able to make a good living for the two of us. Some friends had formed a small Company and it was perfect when they opened their office in the same building where I lived. Things kept getting better for me . . . I could take Kimo to work, with me, downstairs and I sold my first property within a week of getting my license.

I barely heard from Jim but I did hear through the grapevine that he was in trouble. I believe my life was going so well because I was following my heart. I had taken action to get my son to a safe place where we could have a little bliss in between trips to the hospital. At times he seemed better, I lived each day to the fullest . . . but I still knew . . .

My life balanced between Real Estate and Easter Seal School where I would attend weekly meetings with the other mothers of physically challenged children. Danny was a beautiful little five year old boy with big brown eyes and long thick eyelashes. Danny's mom was new to the group and between tears told us of his diagnosis . . . living a life where he would never walk, talk or play. She said that I was lucky that my son was dying, and that I wouldn't be burdened with taking care of him for years, like her. What she said did hurt . . . It also proved to me, once again, that we shouldn't judge others.

Two weeks later Danny's new doctor said he had been misdiagnosed by his first doctor. He immediately put Danny in the hospital, and Danny ended up passing away within that week. His mother understood why I couldn't attend the funeral. I was glad that I had visited him in the hospital where, at last glimpse, he looked just like an Angel . . .

On the move again

I didn't have a car and I had found that Waikiki was the easy place to sell real estate because of the bus system. I put the word out that I needed to move to Waikiki, It happened like magic . . . one of the other agents had a client who wanted to rent his Waikiki condo out which had an ocean view and was right on the bus line. In the mean time I had found several wonderful babysitters who loved Kimo and he seemed to love them, too.

Just before we moved from downtown to Waikiki someone jumped from the roof committing suicide, a thought that I had contemplated at one time, when I was so sad for my son. I was really thankful, now that I hadn't taken my life. Life is just that . . . downs are always followed by ups. It seems that the lower you sink, the forces will come along and present you with an extreme up again . . . you just have to hang in and go with the flow.

I poured myself into work I actually was trying to separate myself from my son, somewhat, knowing that eventually our separation would be final.

One of the agents in the office wanted to get rid of his old car and get a new one, so he gave me a good deal on his car "Thunder". Funny how things turn out . . . from no car and now I was driving a Cadillac, just like Jim, except that his was quite a few years newer than mine.

I could drive Kimo to the beach, once again . . .

CHAPTER THREE

Birth of an Angel

Stepping back to the night my Son was born: It's important for readers to know the depth of my fear of death . . . before I attended the Death and Dying workshop. That night had seemed almost surreal . . . as I lay having contractions several months early. What I had looked forward to as my little bundle of Christmas joy was now arriving the first week in November, really premature.

That morning my water had broke but my Doctor didn't seem overly concerned which really should have concerned me, but I waited as he recommended, to check into the hospital that evening, if nothing happened during the day! My Obstetrician arrived at the hospital shortly after myself to let me know that they were inducing labor and that the baby might not make it and then he left.

This was my first time in a hospital, except when I was born, but I was much too young to remember. My first time giving birth . . . no one present, I was becoming very alarmed! The nurse had checked me, said it would be hours, she then left my room, but I knew that now was the time! What about my baby and what about me . . .

What about my husband downstairs, fresh from the bar watching his favorite football game? I really began to wonder about God . . . where was he?

Realizing it was time, I struggled from the bed to get help! I had made a pact with myself that I would not be screaming as I had seen so many times on TV and in the movies. Barely able to maneuver myself, a frantic nurse passed by realizing my situation, then began yelling instructions for a gurney and shrieking "this one's having hers like a bat out of hell" . . . words that were somewhat unprofessional as well as devastating.

Little did she know that this bat which she spoke of, was indeed headed for a bitter sweet year in the intensive care unit at children's hospital . . . I was rushed into the delivery room just in time! It's amazing when you are faced with a painful situation, both physically and from the heart how you can put yourself aside and outside of the moment and not feel any physical pain.

Gasping for oxygen in between meeting new doctors, nurses and bearing a child, I was too scared to feel pain; even the episiotomy without anesthetic was painless. One final push then the Doctor flashed my Son before my eyes, blue from lack of oxygen, but still he was the most beautiful baby I had ever seen! I felt a rush of pure Love that I had never experienced in my life, realizing at that precious moment I had closed Love out of my heart long ago . . . along with God but now it was back . . .

My beautiful new born Son was rushed to Children's Hospital and I was told that he had a 25% chance to live, if he made it through the night . . . I was rushed to a "holding area" where a mother was demanding and crying to see her baby and very quickly they brought her new "pink" baby . . . to her which was traumatic for me and I could barely hold back my tears . . .

I then overheard a nurse briefing the staff of my son's condition and to "get her out of there" as soon as possible. They wanted me in a private room so that I couldn't hear or see the other mothers with their healthy babies.

I had trouble maintaining myself until I was finally wheeled to my own room to silently cry and pray for a miracle which came in the morning when I received word that he had survived the night! I was ecstatic! Besides the miracle news, I also received a beautiful bouquet of flowers from Jim's office, along with a card signed by the staff.

From one Hospital to Another

I checked out of my hospital and headed for my newborn son's hospital along with his father. No one could ever have prepared us for what we saw in the ICU. (Intensive care unit) We first saw our tiny little baby attached to a respirator, monitors, assortment of tubes, bandages, needles and in this case our new miracle baby weighing in at less than two pounds, lying in an incubator. The good news was he was no longer blue, instead he was yellow! Jaundice, we were told, was common in preterm babies and not to worry about that. I was on overload when we left for the night.

The brutal truth began slowly sinking in with each passing day . . . the odds were getting better for now we were up to a 75% chance if he made it through the next night. These were the times that a doctor's success was measured by survival of patients which was my focus. I had no idea of what future consequences might occur as time went on. Hawaii was one of the last places to gain access to computers so it was difficult to gain access to current medical technology . . . in other words you couldn't just "Google up" the latest information on anything.

My saving grace were the nurses who kept me informed of Kimo's conditions. To this day one of them is my best friend, Sandee. She is the first nurse I remembered . . . I don't know that she was the first I met because at a time like that when you are so overwhelmed with everything, it's hard to remember anything.

My heart ached knowing he didn't stand much of a chance.

I was so grateful when I next saw Sandee on duty for I could see that she was a very good nurse, professional, good natured and could put me at ease as my life fell apart. She shared with me that she had lost her little sister at a very young age. It had been a very traumatic experience for her and one which brought tears to her eyes. I could feel her compassion for both me and my son.

I could barely remember anything but that his lungs were under developed and likewise, his esophagus. These were the two major concerns at the moment. I think they called it Esophageal fistula with a blind pouch, in other words his esophagus was not completely developed and was not connected to his stomach, so he was unable to eat through his mouth, a stomach tube was used for now. The Doctors agreed that there was an operation which could be performed after he gained weight.

He did have all ten fingers and all ten toes which was a good thing. He could wrap his entire hand around my small finger. The operation would have to wait until he weighed four pounds . . . no one knew when that would be.

The Aunties

Because it was Hawaii, the entire staff of nurses became Aunties, Auntie Sandee, Auntie Anne, Auntie Joy, and so on. There was a little boy from Molokai who called the Doctor's, "Daddy". He had been there for a very long time and the staff was working hard, with him, to call his own father "daddy" . . .

All the nurses were wonderful to me and took me under their wing, cheering me up when I was down. They were my support and I wonder if nurses of today realize the importance of their roll to their patients and family. One smile or a word of encouragement can make all the difference in the world. The nurses became my friends but they never over stepped their professional confidentiality rolls.

Our goal: the major operation of attaching Kimo's esophagus to his stomach so that he could eat by mouth and not through a stomach tube. In the interim there were lots of challenges. At one time the Doctors thought Kimo had a hole in his heart, that he had pneumonia, that he might be partially blind, or that he might be deaf. For months there were setbacks and soon the staff would only share the latest reports with me and not Jim, who was having a really hard time accepting it all. Our life at home became more strained but business at the office was booming!

One morning the phone rang at 5:30 am and I was afraid to take the call but someone had to. It was a really nice Japanese Doctor but this morning he seemed very upset. He spoke quickly in broken English and I could barely understand anything he said, except, that Kimo died . . . then he followed up by saying he was okay now . . .

I got so that I would call the hospital for an update in the morning. I needed to mentally prepare myself in advance so that I could put on my happy face for our visits. I could actually recognize the sound of Kimo's respirator on the phone. One morning I called and couldn't hear it . . . by the time the nurse reached the phone I thought they had lost him and didn't want to tell me . . . instead the news was good . . . he had been weaned from the respirator which meant that his lungs were better and that he was getting stronger.

He was putting on weight now and a decision regarding his operation was once again being discussed. It did my heart really good the day I walked in and the nurses had him out of his bed and swinging in his jolly-jumper and he was laughing. This was a big sign of progress, My tears were from happiness and I was filled with hope, once again.

Its Operation Time

He was doing so well that the surgeon scheduled the operation and finally the day arrived. It was one of those days where you are so excited, but try not to be, or show it. A day that you've been waiting for, some six months, a three hour operation that may take five hours. After five hours of waiting, quietly praying, we were told there was a complication but that he was doing okay, then finally after eight hours the surgeon emerged from the operating room coming to me with a big smile and a hug, so now we knew he'd made it through the operation . . . he'd fought for life once again, and won . . . relief . . .

It was some time before I got to see him and to my horror it was as shocking as the first moment I had seen him in intensive care. I hadn't expected to see blood, and so many bandages and tubes . . . I couldn't even take him in my arms to hold and comfort him. I could feel that this had been a major setback, and not what we had hopped for. I still had no idea what the consequences would be. All I could do was try to hold myself together until I got home . . .

Because I was at the hospital almost everyday I saw a lot. I saw deformed, I saw abused children and babies that had died or were in the process. I recognized the "color" of death. One day I was rocking Kimo when a couple came to the door to see their new baby and were told he had expired but because they spoke very little English, they didn't understand what it meant . . . until that day I had only heard the expired word used in context with magazine subscriptions.

As time went by Kimo didn't gain weight like he should have and I learned that if his head didn't reach a certain circumference, his brain wouldn't develop to it's potential and he would never be normal . . . another huge blow to me . . . but I remained optimistic.

Had we made the right decision to go ahead with his operation? This was a question I asked my self over and over. My hind sight has always been better than my foresight. I thought of myself as a really good mother who loved her son dearly, but, had I made the right decision?

There was one day when I had just arrived at the hospital to hear an announcement over the PA system regarding a code, which sent all of the staff rushing in one direction. I asked a new nurse what the code meant and she replied that it was a coronary arrest . . . I asked who, but I already knew. I was so thankful when they revived him, once again.

Arriving at home I was in tears, as usual, my life was a mental hell with all the ups and downs. I thought that all I wanted was to die. What did I have to live for with my nine month old son in intensive care from the day he was born, dying multiple times, I was sickened to witness it just once, never the less each time that I heard he had been coded, was just as heart wrenching as the next. Everything became more than I could take, plus my marriage was "on the rocks" and headed for divorce, I contemplated suicide. I decided the easiest way out would be to go off the Lani which was twenty-seven stories up. I had heard that you would pass out long before reaching the bottom so I would never know, or experience the pain. I wished I was dead . . .

Blinding Explosion

Upon entering the kitchen I noticed a bright light in the upper-oven burner, curious, I put my hand on the oven door to open it, when a voice in my head literally shouted "Don't open it" and at that exact instant there was a huge explosion inside the oven, everything went black! "Thank God I'm alive" was my first thought, then I thought I was blind, but blind seemed much better than dead.

It seemed an eternity before I could see again, but probably it was more like an hour, just long enough to do a reality check on myself . . . how self-centered of me to be so concerned with only my problems. My actions regarding care of my son should have come first . . . I would have missed many wonderful times, before he passed on. I was glad to be alive and it was certainly something I'd never wish for again . . . which I haven't.

The following day when the repair men came to fix the oven they couldn't believe the damage. It was so severe that it caused the rubber between the safety glass to melt completely. The men stated that a burner usually burns out and rarely explodes. They added that I was very lucky because if I had opened the door I would have been killed.

I was most fortunate in heeding to the warning voice inside my head that shouted "Don't open it" and I'm not sure if it was telepathy sent via an Angel or Spirit guide, but definitely, it was from the other side, the invisible God side.

Stepping forward in time: Years later I was honored to have attended a presentation by Matthew D. Dovel, Author of *My Last Breath*. He had died twice, the first time entering the gates of Heaven and the second time he journeyed to Hell.

Matthew was twelve the first time he died. He drowned in a swimming pool while playing with friends. He saw his life pass before his eyes which I can relate to, having my life flash before me at age 19 when I was heading for a horrible car wreck. I was able to gain control of the car at the last second so I didn't reach the light, but Matthew went on to become engulfed in a brilliant white light. He had no previous bible training but he was met by

Jesus . . . and felt he had always known him. He had never felt so good, a feeling of true bliss, but he was told that he had to go back, as he had work to do . . .

The second time he died at twenty-five years of age while committing suicide. He had made some bad choices, but this would be the worst, there would be no bliss for he was headed towards an entirely different destination . . . straight to Hell.

His story is so compelling and his descriptions of hell so vivid that you realize he had to have visited there and that it's not a place that you, nor I, want to go. You can visit his web site at www.mylastbreath.com to see a video that was on Good Morning America. I highly recommend his book to anyone questioning life after death.

You've no doubt heard the old saying that "the third time's a charm" . . . I believe that his third will be better than his first time. He certainly has redeemed himself for past mistakes and done so much work in the area of Suicide prevention and helping others, since coming back. He deserves the best that death has to offer . . . Heaven.

Stepping Back

Stepping back in time: back to Children's Hospital in Honolulu . . . the most unbelievable thing I witnessed was a beautiful little girl who had been brought into the unit after a brain operation and was in a coma. While operating the surgeon had found a massive tumor and ended the surgery. The mother requested that she be kept alive until her father could fly from the mainland to see his daughter alive, one last time.

This is when I witnessed that people in a coma can hear what their loved ones are saying because her father came in and sat next to her bed, he began speaking. I tried not to listen but after a while his final words to her were "I Love You" he kissed her cheek, squeezed her hand and walked to the door . . . the second he closed the door behind himself she died. Her Heart monitor instantly stopped . . . what I witnessed was truly incredible . . .

I believe this little girl's Soul stayed in or around her physical body so that her father could come to say goodbye and "I Love You". I shall never forget that day . . . I should have learned then, that there is life after death.

Kimo's first birthday rolled around and keeping in the Hawaiian tradition we celebrated by hosting his baby Luau at our recreation room by the pool . . . business associates, friends, doctors and nurses all joined us in celebration with Hawaiian music, Food and drink. It would have been a perfect night except that Jim had too many Mai Tai's and told a couple of people off which upset and embarrassed me to the point of tears. After a good time by most . . . It was back to the ICU for Kimo . . .

Kimo was officially released from the hospital and came home a month later to the haunted Condo. We had a resident ghost which hung out by the kitchen and sometimes in the hallway. One of my friends had seen it several times so we made plans to trap him and after that neither one of us saw him again. What would we have done with a trapped ghost anyway?

One of the neighbor's was used to seeing her ghost by the kitchen and hallway. She lived about ten stories below. From one lanai I could see the Ilikai Marina which is where I saw a UFO several years later. A phenomenon seen by hundreds . . . three giant flying saucers which disappeared as quickly as they appeared . . .

From the other lanai I could see punchbowl crater . . . which is where we bought a condo after Jim was given notice to vacate our haunted condo. It all started with a fight during Christmas dinner with his buddy. They fought their way out to the lanai where it appeared that each would throw the other over the railing to the ground far below. The Mele Kalikimaka brawl escalated to shouting and name calling which prompted the neighbor Moby Dick, to call the police who arrived at our door . . . I believe it was when Jim referred to the neighbor as "Moby Fat" that the decision for us to leave the premises was made . . . again, I was completely embarrassed by Jim's antics.My final decision to leave him was mentally addressed. It took almost two years before I could take action but it all worked out for the best . . . how time flies when you're having fun . . .

Chapter Four

Another time and place

It was July and it was a perfect day to hangout at the beach, which Kimo and I both loved. He had been in and out of the hospital for the past four years but I had the staff's permission to check him out and head for our favorite place whenever I chose. Doctors and Nurses were okay with this since everyone was aware of our situation.

This day felt different. We drove out to the North Shore and settled on the warm sandy beach, me on my sand mat with my son contently swinging in his jolly jumper, which I had carefully hung from a tree branch. What had started out as a gorgeous day full of sunshine began to change later in the afternoon when clouds began drifting in. It wasn't long before the sky was soon covered with dark clouds; the sky became black then quickly turned into a torrential downpour!

I packed up very quickly and we raced to the car! I had all sorts of trouble starting *Thunder,* one of those huge, older model Cadillac's that no one wants. After a half hour or so we were on our way except for loud backfires and the constant stalling of the engine the entire way back to the hospital.

The forever tailpipe popping and forward thrusting was quite comical, considering the circumstances. Both of us were in tears from laughter. At one point I looked into his beautiful little blue eyes and somehow I knew this would be our final trip to the beach. Thoughts of Elisabeth's workshop came to me . . . she had spoken of saying goodbye to our loved ones, that we needed to let them go when it's time, and not hold them back.

I began by telling him how much his fathers loved him . . . both, the one here on earth and the one in heaven . . . and I told him how much I Loved him . . . but that if it were his time to go home to God . . . it would be alright and I would be just fine, although I would miss him with all my heart . . .

The storm was becoming worse and at one point it looked as if we'd be stranded in the flooding water, for at one point, we became stalled and stuck in the middle of the road when out of no where a speeding military jeep came up from behind and miraculously missed hitting us. I wasn't quite sure how we were going to get back. My tears were no longer from the back firing, instead they were from shear fear. It was Kimo's giggles that got this mom through the storm, his smiles and a car full of Angels . . . we finally reached our destination.

Darkness looms

It was dark when I dropped him off at the hospital in the pouring rain, with a hug, kiss and a big "I love you Honey-bunny". Had I known the looming call I would be receiving four or five hours later I would never have left him.

Thunder and I finally made it to a gas station a few blocks from home where the engine died for it's final time. I tried to crank it over but there was no way . . . it just wouldn't start . . . I was glad to leave the thing in the middle of the flooding parking lot, thankful that Kimo and I had made it back from the beach safely!

It was after 1:00 am when I got the call, the most dreaded call that a parent can ever receive. The Doctor was from a foreign country and really couldn't speak good English, most likely didn't have a heart; "your Son, he died you know" and of course I didn't know, then she asked if I wanted an autopsy, which ripped me to pieces. The dying scenario I had heard five times before. I was in denial and really didn't want to believe what I was hearing, but, I did have that gut feeling which told me that this was the last time!

I couldn't go to the hospital because of the storm and Thunder . . . Divine Intervention. God had spared me the grief of witnessing that moment . . . the one I had spent preparing myself for, for over five years. The Doctors and nurses loved him so I knew he wasn't alone at the time he died. I also knew he would be surrounded with love on the other side.

I was numb . . . trying to get my thoughts together I stepped out on my lanai which faced the Hilton Hawaiian Village. To my amazement the Rainbow Tower lights formed the sign of a cross which in itself was unusual . . . a true sprinkle from divinity, to have appeared at that moment. A Feeling of peace came over me and I knew that my Son was by my side. I could feel his presence off and on in the weeks that followed . . . what seemed really unbelievable was, that, I also felt when he was away from me that he was somewhere over Australia. This back and forth, near me, then over Australia thing went on for months.

For now, my mind was racing . . . if I could have changed one thing I would have chosen another father for my child, he was not the best father in the world. He did love his son very much, so I won't take that away from him, but he hadn't been there to give us the support we both needed, leaving me to deal with most of the pain.

It was then that I remembered the excitement of Kimo coming home for the first time. Several of his Auntie Nurses had brought him for a few hours so that he could check out his new home. He seemed to understand what we were talking about and laughed along with our jokes. A few weeks later after I had been given CPR instructions and given a short course on his meds He came home with my highest hopes. I actually thought he was going to start talking and walking at one point . . . my hopes soared . . . but there were too many setbacks and too many trips to the hospital to come! It was a very long night . . .

Reality Sets In

I could not shake the feeling that Kimo was here by me and at times over Australia . . .

The following morning the mechanic informed me that nothing was wrong with my car!

My friend Mary was a blessing . . . It is said that "God in his wisdom and his love very often sends his angels down to walk with us, we know them best as "friends" . . . today I was more torn than I'd ever been in my entire life and needed a friend. It was a time that I wished more than anything that it was yesterday . . . Kimo and I would be at the beach, that he would still be alive but at the same time I was deeply relieved that any physical pain was now over for him.

I glanced at the Rainbow tower and although the cross was gone I felt my son's presence was here, with me. I heard Auntie Mary's soft tapping at the door. She had come to drive me to the funeral home.

Everything was all a blur, I felt weak, knowing there were so many arrangements to be made. A twinkle in Auntie Mary's eye, and a smile as she handed me a tiny bottle of wine, the kind they serve on airplanes. Neither of us spoke as we were each at a loss for words. Once in the car she handed me a special poem which she offered to read during the memorial, which I read and we both shared our tears.

I had never been to a funeral or a funeral home before so I had no idea what to expect. I was further saddened, shocked back into true reality to see his little body. My heart ached more than ever and I wasn't sure how I could hold so many tears, but I soon found out. We waited for his father to arrive so we could sign papers then Mary left for her office and Jim and I worked on final details. We went to the print shop and ordered baby blue keepsakes with Kimo's picture on the outside and on the inside was Mary's poem, Heaven's Very Special Child.

Time had no meaning . . . nothing had much meaning and the funeral was over before it seemed to begin. What I remember most was walking towards the beautiful little stained glass chapel in the midst of sugarcane fields. I could hear the beautiful Hawaiian music and as I stepped inside I caught a glimpse of the tiny white casket now open, draped with a beautiful, eighteen foot long, double Red Carnation Lei, and standing next to it was a group of local guys playing lovely music on their ukuleles, and I remember seeing Auntie Sandee with her step son.

I remember Auntie Mary reading her poem . . . "A meeting was held quite far from earth, It's time again for another birth . . . Said the Angels to the Lord above . . . This special child will need much Love . . . His progress may be very slow, accomplishment he may not show, and he'll require extra, from the folks he meets down there . . . He may not run, or play . . . his thoughts may seem quite far away,..in many ways he won't adapt . . . and he'll be known as handicapped, so let's be careful where he's sent . . . we want his life to be content, please Lord, find the parents who will do a special job for you . . . They will not realize right away the leading role their asked to play, but with this child sent from up above, comes strong faith and richer Love, soon they'll know the privilege given in caring for this gift from Heaven . . . their precious charge from so meek and mild, Is Heaven's very Special Child.

Everyone began leaving so when I thought I was the last person in the chapel. I walked to the front for my last glimpse and gave him my last kiss on his forehead turned and walking away everything seemed in slow motion with everyone catching that final glimpse. It was the saddest day of my life and I wasn't sure that I could walk without my legs giving out. I felt so sad and sick but at the same time I was happy that so many had come to pay their respects and offer their blessings in honor of the special child, whom we all loved.

The Magic Apple

Afterwards, Jim and I sat in the limo with Kimo, his little casket stretched across our laps . . . at the last minute I had put his favorite bath toy in the coffin with him, his Magic Apple, which began to chime, as soon as we started driving, and continued chiming at every bump and corner from Mililani to Punchbowl Crater . . . though it was a sad time it's like the Angels were sending a message . . . I could still hear him laughing in the tub, with every chime . . . and although I could not hear his laughter, I knew it was there . . . in another dimension which human ears can't hear.

The cemetery had originally been shaped in the form of a human heart. There had been no choice in the burial location . . . that was left up to the park officials who had designated his final resting place, and we would not know until we arrived . . . I was so surprised to see the awning stretched over an open grave in the center of the heart, where we held a short intimate ceremony.

It was a true blessing and an honor to be laid to rest in the midst of so many fallen heroes who had fought so bravely for our country. I will always think of Kimo as the littlest soldier, for he had bravely fought for his life . . .

It was a year later that the office personnel at the cemetery, shared with me, that there had been more requests to visit his gravesite, than any other grave in the cemetery . . . this helped to heal my heart . . .

CHAPTER FIVE

Soul Magnetism

How powerful the soul is in remembering! You can feel that magnetic attraction in an instant when you stand before the soul of someone you've loved during another lifetime. It isn't meant for us to remember, know or understand what it is at the time. It just is what it is . . .

I was looking into the most beautiful blue eyes I'd ever seen, framed with the most gorgeous thick, curled eye lashes. I wondered why God gave these divine eyes to a man rather than a woman. He had this totally great Aussie accent. And what was peculiar is that I knew what he was going to say before he spoke. I actually could read his mind although I didn't know him. My thoughts drifted back to the night my son died and the months following when I felt his spirit drifting between Hawaii and Australia.

This whole thing seemed so bazaar, it's like I wanted to say at times "you don't have to talk because I already know what you're going to say" but I did like to listen to his accent and he did have a great sense of humor! I believe through several past life regressions where I was his wife who died in child birth, another life he was my Son, another he was a powerful man of the church, which could explain why I understood his feelings and could anticipate the what, when and the how of his thinking.

When he was in town our friends, he and I would hang out on Waikiki Beach in front of the Rainbow Towers or by the lagoon. One day he arrived at the beach in his new swim suit . . . a present from his two children . . . It matched mine exactly, turquoise, purple with a touch of yellow and even the fabric was the same. I'm not sure the meaning of this coincidence but it was kind of fun wondering how that all happened from half way across the world.

Rose Colored Glasses

He wondered often if we as parents view our children through rose-colored glasses and I assured him that we do! I knew he was one of the best, if not the best father in the world . . . He would show me the latest toys he bought for his two children. He always put a great deal of thought as to what the kids could learn from that particular toy, without knowing that it was for learning, but thinking it was just for fun.

He would tell me stories about them which I loved hearing, it seemed to help lessen my own grief. I knew that he was also very sensitive, just as I knew some of his thoughts and mostly what he would say before he said it. The first time I pointed up at Punchbowl Cemetery and told him about my son I noticed a few tears trickling down his cheek . . . other than that, we had many a good laugh.

By some amazing coincidence I knew when his child would be born. I guessed the birth date and the time of birth as he wrote it down being that he was some what skeptical, knowing I could read him like a book. I also knew it to be a boy, which was long before technology allowed us that information.

It was months later that I saw him on the beach. He had my written prediction with him and it was exactly right, to the minute . . . He had to admit that I was right, but he was also a little too pragmatic to admit that it was anything but what it was. I have never had an experience in knowing someone so well, before or since. This information had definitely come to me from some invisible forces . . . I wasn't sure if it were from my spirit guide

It was a few years later that my friend gave up his travel to the islands so that he could be a better father and spend more time attending ball games and such for his children. He had mentioned on more than one occasion how different his last child was from the others. The first two were home bodies . . . this one was like me. He had developed a very free spirit and was most independent, from the time he was a baby. Was it possible that my son's soul had incarnated into the physical body of this man's child, even he wondered.

All Things Are Possible

Since this all happened more than twenty years ago there have been many books written about the subject. These things are possible . . . with parents and children finding each other incarnated in this life . . . I just don't know if I'm ready to find my mom as a child . . .

He said it would be the last time coming to Honolulu. He gave me a business card with his email on the back. Computers were practically nonexistent in the islands at that time, I had no email address however I did tuck his card away.

I made many moves after that, back to Maui, again to Honolulu, to Los Angeles, Marina Del Rey, Redondo Beach, Santa Barbara and then Las Vegas. After living in Las Vegas about seven years I ran across his business card which I found in a stack of old business cards which were bundled with a rubber band. I couldn't believe I still had it after all the years and all the moves. By now I had email so I emailed him just for the heck of it. He was still with the same company, and traveling once again.

He was planning a business trip to Honolulu and I already had vacation plans to Waikiki so we met for lunch at the Royal Hawaiian. I could still read his mind. My childhood dream had been to move to Hawaii from the time I was nine years old. I had started dreaming of my move when I had seen my step-dad's old movies and photos, at a time when there were only three hotels on the beach; the Royal Hawaiian was one of them . Dreams do come true . . .

Something quite out of the ordinary happened in the year that followed; for no known reason, I received an advertisement from the Australian Lottery . . . from the exact Post Office Box number in Sydney, that matched my Son's gravesite number in Honolulu. Of course, I entered my name in the lottery and I did win, even though It was a small sum, it was a way for the invisible forces to get my attention! I guess it was their way of letting me know they are always there for me and that I am right where I should be.

Shortly afterwards I got a card from the Australian lottery with Penguins on it . . . reading *Birthday wishes from Australia* . . .

Through my research, there's plenty of proof that we do travel, through the ages, in Soul families, which helps me to understand the feeling of my Son being near me and over Australia when he died. It also explains how I could read the mind of someone from half way around the world and know what I knew. I choose not to pursue that area because many earthly souls aren't ready for that knowledge . . .

I had been very skeptical about reincarnation until my OBE proved differently and that's at the end of chapter one. Since then my research has shown many well educated and famous people including scientists, have known and believed in reincarnation. Benjamin Franklin, Jack London, Mark Twain, Napoleon, Leo Tolstoy, Henry Ford, Mahatma Ghandi, Ralph Waldo Emerson, Carl Jung, Walt Whitman, General George Patton, Albert Schweitzer, Socrates, and Voltaire, just to name a few of the believers.

A question for the skeptics and scientists who don't believe in this mumble jumble, another rather interesting coincidence; I got an email from: "the little Penguin" Subject: "Celebrate a birthday, adopt a penguin and more" . . . "the little penguin is growing up" and this I received on my friend's son's birthday. This is the son that I had guessed his date and time of birth so many years before. How did I know?

I had a good laugh, knew it was a sprinkle from Divinity. Was it also a validation that I was right about my son's incarnation?

About a year ago I was helping a friend make vacation plans in Hawaii which made me think of my blue-eyed friend so I sent him an email with a photo of the Hilton Hawaiian Village lagoon, immediately he responded back with a photo of the lagoon . . . Unbeknown to me he and his family were on vacation staying at a hotel on the other side of the lagoon. My image and his photo were almost identical. More proof showing our human connection . . .

Another interesting sprinkle from the divine . . . unexplainable by all earthly odds, the day I picked some clothes up from my dry cleaners. I had been going to the same cleaners for five years so they knew my name. After arriving home I noticed the plastic tag was wrong. The last name on my tag wasn't mine . . . It was my blue-eyed friend's last name . . . mere coincidence . . .

Visits from heaven, by Josie Varga, is a wonderful book full of messages from spirits. After witnessing, in person, some of the messages that well known Mediums receive from the other side, this is just more validation that life continues on after death. If there is still any doubt in your mind, she gives more information about books, emails and websites.

What I find interesting is that Josie started her search with a story of Dr. Elisabeth Kubler-Ross which she writes about in her introduction. She couldn't have started her search any better way . . .

CHAPTER SIX

YU and other GOD WINKS

One of my favorite author's Squire Rushnell, has a particular eloquence with words and coins the phrase Godwinks when describing how the power of Coincidence guides our lives. While browsing through one of my favorite bookstores I bought a book on coincidence, but, as I was leaving the shop I felt an incredible nudge to go back inside and I honestly don't know how I had missed *When God Winks* the first time around. There it was as plain as day . . . waiting for me . . . I read that awesome little book from cover to cover that night.

I was so inspired that I sent Mr. Rushnell a letter describing my little "chain of coincidences" and was I ever so surprised and deeply honored when I quickly received a handwritten note back from him thanking me for taking the time to share my story. Now this is a very busy man taking his time to acknowledge me.

He had been an executive with ABC Television Network for over twenty years and had led Good Morning America to the number one position. He went on in his note to say "Isn't it comforting to know that God winks have been mapping your paths all along? Good wishes and continued God winks long into your future." He was right, those winks continue to happen constantly and always have. I just didn't pay attention when I was young, too busy playing and thinking about boys.

Squire writes one fascinating God wink after another about a variety of famous people, sharing his own life full of God winks, from landing his first job to finding the woman of his dreams. He provides guidance to discovering the winks in your life merely by keeping an open mind to all possibilities that you have never imagined. He pretty much covers all walks of life and relationships, history, corporate, and sports which brings me to his perfect golf story, one about a God wink which involves a hole-in-one.

The dream of every golfer is that hole-in-one and after thirty-nine years it finally happened, but even more amazing upon arriving at home this divinely happy golfer found a birthday card from his son which had been mailed four days before . . . fore to golfers meaning to watch out ahead . . . another God wink. What first got his attention was the logo on the back of the card, hole-in-one, but it gets better! The front of his card showed a golfer-guy putting on the ninth green which just happened to be the same hole, the number nine, where this lucky golfer got his hole-in-one earlier that day.

Having worked with groups of golfers through the years In Hawaii, California and Nevada, I find most intriguing the immense camaraderie among them. It's almost like a religion, without a church, but where the word God is spoken a lot.

First Class Golfers

My job at the First Class Lounge in the Las Vegas International Airport gave me the great opportunity to work with many golfers as they love the countless numbers of golf courses in the Las

Vegas, Henderson area and it also gives them a variety of other recreational adventures to pursue after the eighteenth hole.

One such golfer I had the pleasure of meeting was Eric Yu. He will always stand out in my mind along with his mother Emma, father Dick and his brother Richard. I shall always remember their deep kindness and be thankful for our friendship.

Eric, a tournament golfer and who loved the game was only thirty-nine at the time he had a massive heart-attack and passed away on a golf course in Florida. He was doing what he loved most when he died. He was such a humble man that he never did mention that he had shot eight incredible Holes-in-One! The first one he shot when he was age twelve, during a junior tournament.

Richard was a Professor of Psychology at The University of Hawaii and of course at the mention of Elisabeth Kubler-Ross, he instantly knew about her, having studied her works in college. Sadly he and his family were all living the five stages of dying and grief, that he had been teaching. Because I, and my son had met Elisabeth and I had met Eric, somehow this all seemed to fit together, showing me how connected we all are.

It took a good year before Emma could discuss her son's death and how we, as parents never really get over the death of our child. This wonderful couple took flowers to my Son's Grave at Christmas, cleaned around his site and said prayers for him. This so touched my heart!

One particular morning I was going through papers and such, the kind that you've tossed in a drawer vowing to organize them tomorrow, then you forget about them. Later on you run across things that you'd completely forgotten about, which that day, I ran across two golf items. One was a "putt for dough" ball marker and the other was a promotional cleat tool. Not giving this a second thought except that Eric did cross my mind, I got ready for work.

Guess who just happened to come into the lounge that night? Seems like a coincidence but It had to have come from spirit, Squire would have termed it a God wink, finding the golf marker and tool that very day, my thoughts of Eric and now here were the Yu's. This had been a very lucky day for Mrs. Yu, as usual, and I do believe that Eric helps her out . . .

Once again they had gone and visited my son's grave, this was memorial day in 2008 when they surprised me with three pictures showing the American flag and how they had decorated his site with a lovely fresh flower lei intertwined with a garland of Ti. In the Hawaiian culture Ti is a sacred plant bringing good luck and protection. Mr. Yu has said that they think of Kimo as part of their extended family. How sweet is that? Now there's a lot of divinity . . . the root word meaning Godlike. They have so touched my heart many times.

We spoke of coincidences and how everything happens for a reason. Mrs. Yu thought she had been dreaming at first, but then very much felt the presence of Eric and her mother sitting on the bed at Caesars Palace, talking to her. We spoke of Eric's annual Memorial Golf Event.

Emma asked if I thought Eric might have been trying to let her know he was there the day she'd looked into the fridge for Tabasco sauce for Dick, who wasn't supposed to be eating hot sauce anyway, Doctor's orders! She couldn't find it. Then he looked for it but couldn't find it either. As God winks often happen with fun and unclear messages . . . the very next day without looking for the bottle of Tabasco . . . there it sat in the fridge, on the front of the shelf . . . Not a doubt in my mind that Eric was there.

You have to admit that this next coincidence or God wink truly comes from spirit or the invisible forces whichever you choose to name what it is. I was trying to write Death and Divinity at work during downtime. I had just finished the chapter about my son's burial at Punchbowl, quickly wiping away my tears, at the sound of the door bell, and the arrival of my first passengers . . .

Once again, sprinkles from Divinity . . . I was surprised again . . . the Yu family entered the lounge . . . In fact, I could not believe my eyes . . . They are the expression of the true Aloha Spirit! I can see why Eric chose them as his family . . . a family of Angels.

More Angels

Doreen Virtue, Ph.D., not only resembles an Angel but she maintains an angelic demeanor, as well. She's a wonderful author and an Angel authority who holds multiple degrees.

A fourth generation metaphysician working with the Angelic realms in her writings and workshops. She has over twenty books to her credit and writes that she receives many stories from readers regarding Angels and car incidents.

It's taken me many years to realize that it hasn't been me who deserves my good driver status, but it has been the Angels who were guiding me along the way. I sometimes wonder if they are on standby, just waiting for me to take my place behind the wheel of my car. After living in Hawaii for so many years it was quite an adventure to be back on this Big Island of America, with highways stretching thousands of miles cross country. Experiencing the aftermath of "rock-fever", It was exciting to get into my car and drive everywhere at anytime, hoping to relieve that closed in feeling one often gets from living on a small Island.

I would take many road trips, some were for my work, others when I was looking for work. I drove up and down the west coast three times and then later I drove from southern California, through Arizona, New Mexico, the Texas panhandle, Memphis and then on up to Indianapolis.

Following a temporary job I drove south through Branson into Oklahoma City and then on down to San Antonio, escaping pounding rain, snowstorms, sleet, lighting and hail . . . now and then I was blessed with the warmth and beauty of the sun.

At one time I was caught up in unbelievable thick black clouds which had quickly rolled in to cover a sky which earlier had been blue and filled with sun . . . I had no idea where in heaven's name I was. I became a bit tense as everything around me blackened and I could barely see the road ahead of me. Suddenly a small section of black sky parted exposing a huge bright ray of sun light shining directly upon a small cluster of Mediterranean style buildings. It resembled a biblical scene with just one bright ray of sunshine breaking through the sky, shining onto a beautiful small area of earth. It was as if the forces were trying to get my attention with a message which lead my way out of the dark into the light . . . this enlightened spot turned out to be Unity Village and I did manage to find my way back to Kansas City, Missouri from there.

There was another day in which I was out in the middle of nowhere, but still in Texas, some where between San Antonio and El Paso. The sky became dark and full of frightening bolts of lightning crashing to the ground and bouncing all around me and my little sports car. I truly thought this to be my last day on earth and I know that I couldn't have been driving because I was too busy praying . . . but I eventually I made it back to southern California from there.

Life In The Fast Lane

I've read that if you don't have an accident during a high speed blowout then it is truly an act of God . . . which it was!

Anyone who has driven in Las Vegas traffic can tell you about the constant alcohol, drugsdrugs and road rage that must be dealt with 24 hours a day. After having lived in Los Angeles five years, much of it spent on the LA freeway system. I witnessed a number of bad accidents and had some really close calls. I couldn't imagine any place where the traffic could possibly be worse! At one point, after a close call I emphatically stated to myself "I am done . . . no more freeways for me!"

Today, I was in Las Vegas and running late for my business appointment with Matthew on the north end of town, but I was still tied up in traffic on the south side of Las Vegas, so I opted to take the interstate! This was totally against my intuition, but the weather was beautiful so what could I loose?

Once on the freeway the traffic flow was running quite smoothly, though very crowded, when I encountered heavy construction ahead. There were all sorts of warning signs, including danger zone, right lane closed ahead, lane shifts, followed by a posted speed limit of 35 miles per hour.

I had quite a distance to go so I moved over to the far left hand lane next to the center divider. I glanced in my rear view mirror and spotted a speeding vehicle which was creating a safety hazard for everyone on the road. The car had swiftly changed to my lane at breakneck speed and now was directly behind me! I floored the gas to keep from getting rear-ended and now we were both speeding while still in the core of extensive construction!

Once again I had to floor board the gas to keep from getting hit. He stayed right on my bumper, close enough that he could have hit me at any moment, should I make the slightest error!

At this point I became afraid for my life. Checking my speedometer I found that I was now at 80 miles an hour with him still tailgating, disregarding the two-second rule completely!

I was petrified, wanting to switch lanes, but I didn't dare because of the surrounding traffic!

High Speed Blowout

Suddenly I had a rear tire blow out . . . there was a loud noise, a sudden jerk of the wheel and then momentary loss of control! I really did expect to hear screeching tires, horns or at least feel a collision, but . . . instead everything became deadly quiet! I felt a strange, incredible energy surround me followed by a feeling of complete peace! I was no longer afraid and I also felt as if I had a guardian Angel riding on my shoulders who was protecting me from any harm!

My car seemed as if it were slightly airborne, gliding sideways from the far left hand lanes to the right lane, then quickly descending down an exit lane which somehow appeared from nowhere! By the time I reached the bottom of the incline I was noisily riding on one wheel rim with the tire loudly flip-flopping on the street, however I was in luck or was it by coincidence that a gas station just happened to be on my right! How's that for "Divine Intervention"?

I was not at all familiar with this part of town . . . I got out of my car, at which time a gentleman appeared named Matthew, who offered to change my tire . . . another coincidence!

That's at least "a double-divine Intervention" in my book! He'd seen me come off the freeway and having a wife and daughter of his own, had rushed to my rescue . . .

He quickly changed the remains of the melted piece of black rubber . . . which minutes before had been a tire! With an abundance of gratitude I was on my way . . . as Matthew disappeared with other pedestrians on the nearby sidewalk.

I didn't make it to my meeting with the intended Matthew, but I was destined for a meeting with Matthew and I do know it was a miracle that no one was hurt that day. I was physically sitting in the driver's seat, but at one point it was not I who was doing the driving. Let's just call it an act of God, because I did think this was the end . . . but there is never an end to angels!

The day after I finished writing the above paragraph I was headed to work at the airport, and driving through the airport tunnel. I was in the middle lane of three and as I approached a Taxi to my left and began moving along side of it. A voice in my head whispered "look to your left" which I did, only to see the taxi edging into my lane and into the side of my car had I not swerved quickly out of the way to avoid an impact!

The voice whispered again "look to your left" . . . I realized the taxi driver had not seen me, although my headlights were on, he forced me out of my lane completely, at fast speed almost forcing me into the side of the tunnel! We would have had a serious wreck if

I had not heard, or paid attention to the voice in my head which was a male voice, which indicates that it wasn't my own thought. It's clear that this indeed, was another sprinkle from the forces. Some call it coincidence, but it's more than that . . .

I believe that Angels are not only in cars but also in planes and trains, at least they had to be with me during the train derailment outside of Dallas and also during an aborted landing at The San Francisco International Airport.

Flying High

A friend of mine was flying from Dallas to Kansas City on a very uneventful flight when the Captain came on the public address system announcing that they were on schedule, about 20 minutes from landing and proceeded with details of the remaining trip "rain showers in the DFW area with pockets of chop".

Within a minute of that address my friend felt his life was coming to an end because of a tremendous high voltage explosion in the rear of the aircraft and a pink flash of light which traversed through the cabin, knocking his mind and breathe in complete disarray. There was a great sense of alarm among the passengers with my friend anticipating the nose of the plane to point down or go into some kind of gyration and breakup as a result of the explosion.

What seemed an eternity but probably was more like five seconds the Captain returned to the PA system to inform passengers that they had just been struck by a bolt of lighting and assured them that structurally the plane was fine and that there was nothing to be concerned about. The event had generated a total feeling of powerlessness.

Shortly the guy sitting next to him mentioned something which could have been "Holy something" and then began a fast-speed dissertation about his wife, kids and job . . . he was also glad to be alive after the experience . . . my friend introduced himself as Steve to Ray. Steve says Ray is my first name then Ray said, well my middle name is Steve with a "ph" . . . wow my friend thought we have the same name Raymond Stephen . . . then his next question was a shot in the dark . . . "so what's your last name?"

My friend wasn't sure if the lightning bolt or what he was about to hear were more of a shock when Ray replied Rudy . . . "that's my last name" said Steve . . . talk about being in the twilight Zone so they both reached for their wallets as proof . . . so when's your birthday? My friend Steve asked, December 19th, Ray replied and Steve said in disbelief . . . "that's my birthday." Which all was confirmed, as the two men compared driver's licenses. And guess what? They were both born in 1955 but not in the same city.

The odds of being struck from lightning are relatively high but the rest is rather mind blowing and would never have happened had it not been for "an act of God" . . .

The obvious questions have always remained with my friend Steve: Why? . . . What did it mean? . . . Was it a coincidence? . . . Was it intentional? . . . It's beyond his comprehension but I know that it'll all make sense to him someday . . . God continues to Wink . . .

CHAPTER SEVEN

I Can Do It Too-Louise Hay

So it began . . . The dynamic 2007 "I Can Do It" Hay House conference in Las Vegas, Nevada. You could hear the crystal clear voice of Cecilia singing *The Rose,* which rang throughout the entire convention center. I felt as if I were in heaven listening to an angel sing.

"The soul, afraid of dying that never learns to live" . . . "Just remember the seed . . . with the sun's love in the spring becomes the rose". Cecilia's amazing voice of three octaves, brought tears to many eyes of the thousands in attendance, including Louise Hay.

Louise, the owner and founder of Hay House publishing, humbly took the spot light following a much deserved standing ovation! She resembles the likeness of a Goddess, the healing Goddess, at which time she announces to the audience that she usually doesn't begin by crying . . . and it was truly a heartfelt moment by all. I had read her most famous book, but this was my first time to actually see her in person.

She was then 80 years old and simply radiated in front of the entire audience . . . she continued on saying that she intended to make this decade . . . the best decade of her life! The energy was at an incredible high! I decided that if she can do it, I can do it too. I've never forgotten her words of inspiration and so far it is becoming my best decade. This has become my daily affirmation "This decade is the best decade of my life" . . .

She then shared with us that a new hybrid Rose had been developed and named after her and keeping with synchronicity it just so happens a single rose is my favorite flower. I felt as if I were really in the right place at the right time . . . here among so many positive souls . . . this fabulous weekend had just begun!

Saint Louise

Congratulations were in order to this precious lady for It was the 20th year anniversary of Hay House Publishing and Louise proudly announced the reason for so many cameras throughout the center, that they were there to film the movie of her life, *You can heal your life*. Her story can be read in her international Bestseller by the same name. The Australian Media once dubbed her "the closest thing to a living Saint".

I have witnessed this Saint in action and I must agree with the Aussies, who have dubbed her right. I have seen her standing hours on end at her I Can Do It Conferences . . . greeting hundreds and hundreds of loyal fans with a warm smile and kind words. I have been the recipient of her many kind words. She is my true inspiration.

Her childhood was one of unhappiness, spent enduring both sexual and physical abuse, then running away from home at the age of fifteen. She later moved to New York and became a high-fashion model, divorces, becomes diagnosed with cancer then she miraculously healed her own disease. In Los Angeles she went on to help thousands of AIDs patients by creating the "Hay Ride" which began with only six men in her living room. The word was out and it wasn't long before the groups grew to hundreds.

Jay, a good friend of mine had attended Hayrides in honor of his friends. He was in the film industry, working as a professional hairstylist and makeup artist, and knew many who were being diagnosed with AIDs. He remembers most that Louise would be holding up the mirror in front of those afflicted with the disease, which in the early 80's had manifested by a huge proportion . . . No one knew much about the disease . . . but Louise knew she needed to help . . .

She also knew that you can overcome your own afflictions by loving yourself and that is what the mirror was all about . . . looking in a mirror and telling yourself that you love you . . . then of course you can take that giant step forward into the healing process . . .

In *You can heal your life*, she developed a list of every conceivable illness, followed by the probable cause, and then a healing affirmation . . . She discovered that there are really just two patterns that contribute to disease . . . that is fear and anger. It is up to you who must believe and forgive, and also, forgive yourself. I truly believe this and am blessed with good health. She continues to help so many through her publishing company specializing in self help, inspirational and transitional books.

Many of her Authors and their books have validated what I know to be the truth. What I love are the I Can Do It conferences that her company presents. You can actually meet the authors and have a word with them while they sign their book. Due to my hectic work schedule I was able to see only the keynote presentation of Dr Wayne Dyer in 2006. He absolutely knocked my socks off and also in 2007. His entire keynote addresses are without notes . . . He knows the forces are by his side if he needs help.

Mediums

My first workshop of the day was that of Gordon Smith, an astounding medium from Glasgow, Scotland. This conference was my first time to see mediums. Gordon just happens to be the U.K.'s most accurate medium and has authored *Spirit Messenger*, an intriguing book which will leave no question as to the reality of life after death.

He became so connected with the spirits who had crossed over, that he could actually feel the pain of illnesses and death. He was non stop for over an hour with chest, throat, leg pains, cancer or whatever the spirit crossed over with . . . then he had to stop for a short break . . . all the while displaying his charming sense of humor, especially when a horse came across in the middle of a spirit connection. It happened that this had been a lady who loved horses and her daughter was in the audience to validate everything happening. It was simply amazing to see him pulling all of this out of the air non-stop. Because of the emotions streaming from those whom his messages were intended for, I knew it was real and I knew it was also from the other side.

My next workshop was that of Stuart Wilde, certainly living up to his last name and was totally Wild, funny and fun! He is guaranteed to keep you alert during the entire workshop. I had searched for years regarding Out-of-Body Experiences, but found none that matched mine. In 2001 Stuart and others had discovered a new phenomena . . . very new to me, one which he calls "The Morph". It's an interference pattern that enters a room changing it's nature. the information that an individual gathers from dreams and visions.

Perhaps I had observed the Morph, thinking it was an Out of Body Experience. The Morph hadn't been discovered at that time and Stuart claims that it's information tailored to suit our spiritual evolution through life. He's documented over 30,000 of these visions and has got quite a following of fans. Fans who honored him with a standing ovation, which certainly speaks for itself.

Keeping with all the grandeur that Las Vegas, has to offer, and to the delight of the audience, her Majesty Sylvia Browne was transported on stage in a glitzy Chariot hand carried by two very handsome and extremely muscular Golden Gods, bringing a much deserved standing ovation. She and spiritual intuitive Colette Baron-Reid ended the evening performing amazing readings to audience members.

Earlier in the day I had spoken with two women, who had, had a previous phone reading with Sylvia, who asked about the blue-eyed woman with a heart-shaped face. Believe me, Sylvia could not have seen her daughter over the phone, but her words fit this lady to a tee. There were no other words to describe her heart shaped face . . . I became a believer in Sylvia's psychic abilities that evening.

I have only seen "the soul" in the eyes of half a dozen people in my life but I did see Sylvia's soul after her performance, following her spiritual connections.

"This decade really will be the best decade of my life" . . .

CHAPTER EIGHT

Synchronicity-Dr Wayne Dyer

Manifest Your Destiny was the first book by Dr. Wayne Dyer, that I read, and I read it because at the time I needed quite a few manifestations . . . the company I had been working for, suddenly went out of business so I lost my job, could barely pay rent, eat, and my car was repossessed!

"You have the power within you to attract to yourself all that you could ever want" are his opening words in the introduction. I knew his book had the answers, principles that I had learned, but had forgotten to follow. I had given up on myself and lost trust in myself. This in essence is giving up on God, as well. This was how I had gotten myself into this mess, simply by not believing . . .

I decided to change my thoughts and end my pity party. Shortly before I even finished reading his book I sent a thank-you letter to Dr. Dyer for his wonderful book and expressing my gratitude of how much his words had meant to me.

I was quite surprised and taken back to find a package from Dr. Dyer in my post office box. My post office was directly across from McCarran International airport in Las Vegas and each time

I picked up my mail I silently wished that I were working at the airport. I had spent years traveling and working in and around airports in Hawaii and California. I had reached a point where I was more at home in airports than in my own home.

Dr. Dyer had taken time out of his busy schedule to read my letter and sent me a wonderful gift, his *power of Intention* perpetual flip calendar, which I have read everyday to this day.. March Twenty-Second was the day I received the calendar with a powerful thought for the day:

"Perhaps the surest way to happiness and fulfillment in life is to thank and praise your source for everything that happens to you. Then, even when a calamity arises, you can be assured that you'll turn it into a blessing". Thank you Dr. Dyer.

Amazing things began to happen which appeared as coincidence, but definitely were meant to be. Carl Jung first described this philosophy of synchronicity in the early twenties, which can become mind blowing.

A week later I started working at the airport, in the first class lounge and I began working mainly with Hawaiian Air passengers, which was so much fun and a blessing, and more coincidence . . . since I had lived in the Islands for seventeen years I was able to greet old friends and make new ones. One of which turned out to be a lady living in the same building where I lived when my son had passed away.

The second week I began at the lounge a previous boss, Frank who was buying a new car, called and asked if I wanted to buy his used car . . . one which was only three years old, and in perfect condition. He also included the auto insurance until I could get on my feet . . . Things were happening and I was excited. Wayne Dyer was right, I did have the power to attract all that I could want, and for now I was thankful and happy to attract the necessities.

It wasn't long before my roommate and I moved from a one bedroom apartment where I had been happy and thankful to sleep on the couch . . . to a larger apartment where I had my own bedroom and bath again. Shortly I moved to an even larger condo, thanks to Frank, once again.

One of the interesting things about the lounge is that it had a resident ghost living there. four of us managed to see him, but of course we didn't mention it to any of the passengers until after he had left the lounge for good . . . He hung out by the departure board a lot, probably waiting for final boarding . . . eventually, he must have caught his flight . . .

He did like television as well as beer. It was interesting that he kept his distance from the two of us that accepted him and weren't afraid . . . but he managed to scare the hell out of the other two that were afraid of him! They heard the door between the bar and supply room start swinging, and one of them took off running then one of them saw him sitting on the couch in front of one of the televisions watching T.V which scared her to no end . . . It was afterwards that no one saw him again.

Six months later I was fortunate enough to take my first vacation in years, to my favorite place Hawaii, and what surprised me most at the last minute, as I was boarding, they put me in first class. I was wearing my swimsuit under my regular black suit. I was one of the first off the plane but, I was the first on the beach, my favorite beach in front of the Hilton Hawaiian Village.

A little over a year after my job had started I had the good fortune of attending the opening night of the "I Can Do It" Hay House conference here in Las Vegas. Dr Dyer was the opening Keynote speaker. His positive energy ignited the entire room the moment he made his appearance walking through the crowd shaking hands and stopping for photos with friends and fans. His amazing energy and powerful message had a way of tugging at the heartstrings of the entire audience once he was on stage.

The evening was over too quickly . . . for I had to leave and go back to work but I have been rather fortunate to attend other I Can Do It conferences where I love listening to his inspirational addresses. I don't know how he speaks without notes.

In *Inspiration . . . your ultimate calling*, he writes that this is the most personal book he's ever written and has chosen to use experiences from his own life that he's experienced firsthand. The book cover shows him holding a beautiful Monarch Butterfly sitting on his hand. This "mystical encounter" takes place while walking a beach on Maui. My favorite island . . . He was recalling an old friend Jack who had crossed over about a decade before. Jack loved Monarch butterflies. Dr Dyer knew this to be his friend jack, who stayed with him for two and a half hours.

Unbelievably the next morning he watched one of his favorite films *brother sun, sister moon* which he hadn't viewed for a decade, the opening scene, life of St Francis shows a butterfly alighting on his fingers . . . Is that not Synchronicity? I think of it as a sprinkle of Divinity giving Dr. Dyer validation that the butterfly truly was Jack . . .

Here's more . . . Stepping back to my job at the lounge which I loved and after five and a half years I lost it . . . absolutely devastated when I found out the new Company would not be keeping me on. By then I knew everything happens for a reason and this certainly did! I've always considered thirteen to be my lucky number . . . my birth date. My last day of work was exactly thirteen years to the day that I moved to Las Vegas. Synchronicity again . . .

I knew that I had now been given the time to finish my book; The book that Elisabeth Kubler-Ross had told me to finish, in my past life regression with Dr Brian Weiss. This is what I was meant to do with my life. For years I had spoken of my book, but I had never found the time to write it. I would now have time . . . destiny was calling me . . .

I thank Dr. Dyer for his many words of wisdom which have given me insight into my life.

It was hard leaving a job I knew and loved, at retirement age, heading out to do what I didn't know how to do! Somehow its all come together . . . I can now help people who fear death, because I know that death does not exist. I hope to contribute to Elisabeth's legacy . . .

CHAPTER NINE

Past life Regression-
Dr Brian Weiss

The 2007 I Can do it Conference continues and. the following day I had signed up for a Past Life Regression workshop. This was a topic I was very skeptical about, but at the same time I was very curious about. I decided to tread the waters of lake skeptical and attend the workshop led by Dr. Brian Weiss. You may have seen him on the Oprah show, more than once. I surmised that since I didn't believe I could be regressed, that I wouldn't possibly be regressed! Believing in reincarnation but being a total skeptic on the process of past life regression, I sat back merely to enjoy and observe the others, feeling pretty comfortable because the doctor had been a skeptic . . . so we had that in common! He was someone who could immediately set you at ease.

Dr Weiss graduated from Columbia University and received a Medical Degree from Yale University School of Medicine, completing his residency in Psychiatry. He was an academic Psychiatrist utterly skeptical about "non-scientific" areas! He did not know the concept of Reincarnation nor had any interest in the subject. He had one client who changed his thinking.

I felt even more at ease when he advised us that we could leave the past life, should we became uncomfortable, just by opening our eyes . . . we could leave the process at any time. He then dimmed the lights, I closed my eyes, listening to his soothing voice and wonderful music to calm the soul.

He suggested at one point to enter a peaceful garden . . . My garden was full of sunshine, pretty flowers and colorful butterflies! I could feel the warmth of the sun and an overwhelming feeling of peace.

He then prompted us to go to another lifetime in another place, at which time I began strolling along a beautiful white sand beach . . . I was barefoot and the surf felt incredibly warm and wonderful! I could feel my long, flowing skirt gently blowing in the breeze.

Off to my left was the most awesome ocean I'd ever seen! The color was a radiant light blue which I have yet to see in this lifetime, then off to my right were green rolling hills with what appeared to be an early Mediterranean style village nestled among the banks.

Dr. Weiss then prompted us to go to a later time in that day . . . It was night, I was a young beautiful girl who joined the tribesmen in one of the casitas for an evening of merriment, entertainment and feasting! We were gathered around an enormous table filled with delectable food and drink fit for a king! Flaming torches provided the only light.

A very handsome man sat down across from me and we began flirting. He was smiling and we were laughing with one another into the wee hours. I felt really happy and asked my friend next to me who this man was and she said "he's the one with the blue eyes" which set him apart from the others. All the men had brown eyes, brown hair and all were tan with extremely muscular physiques.

Dr. Weiss then prompted us to go to our last day in that life and that we would feel no Pain. I momentarily felt that I didn't want to go to the last day but I did so anyway. It was night time and I was laying on a bed of animal hides, the room was dimly lit by torches, and I was surrounded by half a dozen villagers whom seemed to be some sort of doctors and servants. The one with the "blue eyes" had his arms around my shoulders and as he kissed my neck I began floating above my body, higher and higher, just observing myself and the others below!

Slowly I began spiraling up and then I realized I was dying during child birth. I felt no physical pain but what I did feel was a deep sense of LOVE and missing of my husband and Son as I spiraled up and out of that lifetime.

The group was now prompted to return to the garden at which time Dr. Weiss made mention that there would appear a being whom loved us unconditionally! Miraculously a pretty young woman came forth whom I knew to be Dr. Elisabeth Kubler-Ross in this life time.She had brought my attention to this term and also the meaning of unconditional Love at her workshop on Maui, when my Son was dying.

Her message to me was quite strong in that she asked that I carry on her work. Three Times she repeated "Finish your Book!" For months I would struggle with what work she had meant. How could I help carry on the work of this great lady who was so diversified in her career!

Following the regression I was too overwhelmed with emotion to share with the group my experience! My past life was very real filled with a feeling of much happiness and I now felt very sad upon leaving it.

During the book signing, following his workshop, I gave Dr. Weiss a Three-dimensional bookmark which I had designed from my vision and out of body experience the last night of Elisabeth's workshop. Dr. Weiss received it with much grace and acknowledged that he had been a friend of Elisabeth's! This might have seemed a real coincidence, however it was she who first enlightened me to the fact that there are no coincidences, that everything, everything happens for a reason!

This morning as I was crossing the street to the convention center there lay the body of a dead pedestrian in the cross walk! It did not dawn on me that this was a clear sign from the other side regarding my subject matter and Elisabeth's urgent message to "carry on her work" of life after Death!

My past life regression had certainly brought me in touch with my being for this present life, answering many questions regarding the obvious connection and special bond between my blue eyed friend and myself. I believe this regression had touched on my most tragic event of this lifetime, the fear of my son's death, even at birth. The Doctor wasn't sure that he would live. I believe because I had died during childbirth in a past life that my fear carried over to this life.

Although my second regression was a year after the first one . . . I no longer was the skeptic that I had been. I had to take a seat on the floor, my back against the wall because I became relaxed so quickly that I had a difficult time staying in my chair. I was really looking forward to experiencing another life with others from my past. What was so amazing is that I had two short fragments consisting of two previous lives that came forward, with my same "blue eyed friend" from this lifetime!

He was not the father of my child this time, instead he was my child . . . and we lived in London! My sweet little boy kept coming to the windows of the brothel where I worked, and motioned me outside to come play with him. He had a big smile on his face and I felt badly that I had to hide him from my patrons, sadly waving him away each time.

After this incarnation he appeared as a high ranking clergyman of the Roman Catholic church in Italy where we both had to hide our Love for each other. His name was George and he said that he "loved me very much." Several times he repeated this.

Dr. Weiss writes that there is someone special for everyone. Often there are two or three or even four. They come from different generations, they travel across oceans of time and the depths of heavenly dimensions to be with you again. They come from the other side, from heaven. They look different but your heart knows them . . .

CHAPTER TEN

More Syncs and Caroline Myss

Disillusioned with her work as a journalist Caroline was given an assignment to cover a workshop on Death and Dying led by Elisabeth Kubler-Ross. This was the exact type of workshop I attended, in Chapter One, which led to the most profound week of my life.

Caroline Myss Ph.D. is brilliant, a bestselling author, Medical Intuitive and Keynote Speaker writes in her book, Sacred Contracts "it was the level of suffering in that workshop, and the astonishing way that Elisabeth was able to help people devastated by the death of a loved one" which inspired her to return to school and study religion and mythology. She ended her career as a newspaper journalist going on to obtain a Masters degree in Theology.

Caroline writes that our willingness to accept that "everything we do is for a purpose far greater than we will ever know, that every deed you do affects your life and others".

Stepping back for one moment, let me recall a day where synchronicity kicked in at one of my favorite book stores. The following is an example which truly validates Caroline's message to us all.

I was browsing, searching for Caroline's book *Sacred Contracts* without any luck when all of a sudden a small book popped off the shelf landing at my feet! Thinking nothing about this small deed, I picked up the book and as I was placing it back on the shelf I noticed the title . . . *On life after Death* by Elisabeth Kubler-Ross with a new foreword by Caroline Myss!

Although I was disappointed in not finding the book that I had set out to find I was delighted to have found this little treasure . . . I knew that this was no mere coincidence. I rushed home with my precious purchase which I read from cover to cover. That afternoon I had decided that Caroline's book would have to wait for a special time. That time would be far greater and more special than I ever could have imagined . . .

Caroline's foreword honored Elisabeth as "one of the heroines of our age" whom devoted her life to the existence of an after life, one that is beautiful. Identifying the stages of dying made Elisabeth famous—Death did not scare her and that made her one of the most controversial figures of the medical community during her lifetime.

Back to Caroline's book which I had put on hold until a special time. I found it in the city where I was born, San Diego, California. It turned out that Caroline was a key note speaker at Louise Hay's "I Can Do It 2009 Conference", which I was attending. What could be more special than to see and hear her dynamic speech and to find her book, *Sacred Contracts*?

It gets better . . . afterwards she spoke with me personally and then graciously signed both books, a truly special time for me, more so than I had ever thought possible, More so than Caroline could know the impact on my life.

This was more validation that everything happens for a reason. I have found that when I really feel disappointed that if I just hang and give it to God . . . I know that the Universe will always exceed my expectations.

Something else that seems a coincidence, but not really . . . going back to Caroline's Sacred Contracts, page thirty-one, then check out page thirty-one Ronald Mann's Sacred Healing and you will find they both write about attending Elisabeth's workshop and that they were both greatly influenced spiritually by the painful experiences regarding death, that they witnessed.

Pretty amazing that both books mention Elisabeth Kubler-Ross's workshops: on page thirty-one and that both of the book titles consist of two words, that one of the two words are identical, Sacred . . . there are nearly 130 million books in the world . . . what are the odds? I call it sprinkles from Divinity . . .

Both of their careers were greatly influenced spiritually after attending Elisabeth's workshops. Caroline returning to school to study RELIGION and MYTHOLOGY obtaining her masters in THEOLOGY, the science of things Devine. Ron went on to successfully develop and integrate his traditional methods of PSYCHOTHERAPY with Spirituality, becoming a CONSULTANT, KEYNOTE SPEAKER and Personal Coach.

One last significant thing before I end..originally when I was looking for Caroline's book and Elisabeth's little book had popped off the shelf landing at my feet. It was holding a very clear message for me . . . Elisabeth wrote **"my real job and that is why I need your help, to tell people that death does not exist"** . . . although her words were for many, they were most significant to me! During my first past life regression she made it very clear for me to finish my book, she was very adamant three times to "finish your book" . . . see previous chapter . . .

I ask myself why didn't I get this message loud and clear from my past life regression..I should have gotten the clue because this had been the morning I saw the dead pedestrian in the cross walk . . . but we can't always see or figure signs out when they come to us. I like to believe I'm wiser now.

Five years ago if anyone had suggested to me that before we are born we sign a contract on the other side regarding our accomplishments for this earthly life, I wouldn't have truly believed that anything like that would be possible. Now I know that that's all part of it. In other words we have reasons for coming here and once we're done we get to go back home, to the other side.

In *Sacred Contracts,* Caroline can show you how to put pieces of your life together so that you can figure out your purpose in this life and much more. She shows you how to develop symbolic sight and archetypal language in order to grasp your life with clarity. She's simply amazing in the way she brings it all together for us.

Let us not forget that everything happens for a reason and I believe it all goes back to our contracts and that's what coincidence is all about. Is our subconscious remembering what we signed up for, before we came here, then trying to remind us?

Go to www.myss.com where you learn more about her workshops and journeys to spiritual places. You can learn more about CMED. Her institute, internationally recognized, offering seminars on spirituality and human consciousness.

Chapter Eleven

Time Prompt 11:11

It was 11/11/2009, I was headed for the library, not realizing it was closed, nor did I realize it was the 11th day of the 11th month. I decided to go to the book store, always my favorite hangout. There I spotted a book that I wasn't familiar with *11:11 The time prompt Phenomenon* . . . by Marie D. Jones and Larry Flaxman. I had to have the book because I was driving myself bananas seeing these numbers over and over for the past three years.

The authors have researched everything that you could possibly want to know about numbers. I consider them experts, they have each had experiences with time prompts, and write that "Seeing 11:11 on the clock day after day, night after night, is not coincidental. It is not just a random event that keeps repeating. It happens for a reason. Unfortunately, we still don't know what that reason is."

Presently my computer time shows 11:11 as I'm writing this, and believe me it just happens, I don't go around looking for these numbers to be there, as is the same with most eleveners or whom ever we are. What's amazing is that I was waking up at 11:11, glancing at clocks, cell phones, computers, emails, addresses, signs, etc; whether it was 11:11 a.m. or p.m.

At first I thought I was loosing my mind but I now realize It's a way that the invisible forces have of distracting me away from this earthly illusion we call life and pull my thoughts towards another energy . . . I just accept it with a smile and consider it a sprinkle from divinity. I see many 1110, 111, 1001,110, 101 and 11's, as well, as11:11.

A perfect example was the mail I mysteriously received from the Australian lottery with odds better than any lottery here. I rushed out and purchased my $20.00 money order. It was not until I was writing the address that I noticed that the Post Office Box number in Sydney was the exact number on my son's gravestone in Honolulu . . . 1110. By the way, I did win a small amount but it's just interesting and fun to point out that we are talking thousands of miles in distance and thousands of P.O. boxes in Australia.

This morning I am drafting the final copy of Chapter four and have shed quite a few tears because I was writing about the night my son died which was at 1:10 a.m. I had just finished writing the following sentence . . . "I could not shake the feeling that Kimo was here, by me, and at times over Australia" . . . glanced at the time on my laptop . . . which immediately switched from 11:10 to 11:11 a.m . . . . validation from the invisible.

Emails are a great place for the 11:11 to happen and I usually don't notice them until they are forwarded back to me showing the time I sent the original. I once heard one of my favorite 80's songs on the 11th, three times in one day. I've gotten emails sent at 11:11 from my favorite people, which makes me wonder which one of us was the message meant for. Another time my supervisor asked me to close her email . . . it was 1:11 and she had 111 emails in her in box . . .

Wyland the Great

My Post Office Box is located at 1001 Sunset: The last time I was in Long Beach I was at the Hyatt room 1001 which looked directly out on the Whaling Wall by Wyland whom I had the honor to meet in Honolulu when he was completing his first wall in Hawaii. It was on the Ilikai Marina Condominium next to Kaiser hospital. He was told later that several of the cancer patients lived longer because they wanted to see his wall completed. He truly inspired them.

Is it by coincidence that as I've driven up and down the west coast that I should see him high on the scaffolding painting his precious sea life? He does wonderful work for marine life and I find it hard to believe that at many times his great work has become controversial, all the while, he has done so much for the planet. I've been most fortunate to have seen him working on his Whaling Walls in Mission beach, long Beach, Redondo beach, California and also a wall in Newport Oregon.

Go to www.wyland.com to learn more about his clean water challenge and the Wyland Foundation.

Messages from Spirit

Colette Baron-Reid, Intuitive Counselor, speaker and author writes in *Messages from Spirit,* that as long as she can remember 11:11 shows up when she's on the right track . . . according to the time on my computer it's now 11:11 and I had just written the words "Messages from Spirit" . . . how divine is that?

I am honored to have met Colette and to have seen her in action as she accesses the world of Spirit through her humor and sixth sense, which we all have, but most of us don't know how to use it. She has developed her connection to the other dimension and likes us to know that our loved ones still live . . . even though they leave their bodies behind.

She is truly amazing in person and you shouldn't pass up an opportunity to see her if you get the chance. She is also featured on HayHouseRadio.com where she had asked for 11:11 stories from her listeners and she received hundreds of e-mails, too many to be considered mere coincidence.

Continuing my search, I found a most interesting website www.1111angels.com and emailed them immediately. This website group is based in Australia, offering three books written by George Barnard regarding the 11:11 time phenomenon. His third book offers a roadmap for readers who have received the prompt, of which there are over 75 million on the planet.

There are 1,111 Midwayers, whom send us these prompts, according to George. It seems to be a very special group of angels, just waiting to help . . . my computer time it's now 11:10 just flipping to 11:11, again . . . I have to smile . . . It's just Divine with me.

Ellen Degeneres tagged her record label company Eleveneleven and said on her TV show that she named it that because every time she looks at a clock she sees the number 11:11 and whenever she's anywhere she see's the number 11:11 all the time. Kellie Pickler appeared on Ellen's show after her wedding on 1-11-2011, she also says she's an elevener.

In 2007 I pulled up a website called www.december212012.com which gives a countdown in days, hours, minutes and seconds to the end of the Mayan calendar. Four months later I woke up at 11:11 a.m. by the sound of a rustling paper falling from my dresser top, landing next to my bed. This paper was a printout from that website. It was then that I first noticed the time of final countdown on December 21, 2011 is 11:11 a.m. GMT . . . some say it's the end of the world . . .

GMT means Greenwich Mean Time, Greenwich England which is the place where all world time zones are measured from, where time remains the same year round. You can find the website for GMT at www.greenwichmeantime.co.uk where you can find that time in your local time zone.

Chapter Twelve

Stepping Forward:
Bring it on . . . 12-21-2012

12-21-2012 no matter what path we are on, we are all headed here . . . there are no detours . . .

12-21-2012 11:11 a.m. The world comes to an end today . . . so the doomsayers say!

You can actually sign up now to escape death . . . this being at considerable expense, of course. If you go to www.howtosurvive2012. com there's a list of places for best survival odds but you would have to spend most of your money to get there and once you do get there, you will be alone because no one wants to go there, yet.

The following is a list of those possible, survival places: The highlands of Ethiopia, high mountains of Turkey, Madagascar, Atlas Mountains of Morocco, and my choice would be the high mountains of Spain. There's only one problem . . . there's the danger of nuclear-fallout . . .

All the Budget information is included on the site along with information about the places of least survival possibilities of which the United States, Canada and Australia are on the list.

My Agenda

I'd rather choose former aerospace computer systems designer, Gregg Braden's formula, from his, *The Divine Matrix,* then combine it together with Barbara Marx Hubbard's Synergy Engine and go with this agenda. Barbara an author, speaker, futurist and once nominated for vice-presidential candidate and who had proposed a new social function: a Peace Room . . . has my vote!.

I was fortunate enough to attend a dynamic workshop of Gregg's, who's considered an authority of bridging the wisdom of our past with today's science in order to create peace for the future. He certainly caught my attention when he showed us a short preview to the movie *2012* a year prior to the movie's release. I saw the full length movie twice, each time reminding my self this was just a movie meant to scare the hell out of movie goers . . . which it does.

The End of Time

"We're living the end of time. Not the end of the world". His words bring peace of mind in his introduction to *Fractal Time.* For over 20 years Gregg has scoured the remote areas of Egypt, Peru and Tibet to uncover secrets of the past which show beyond any doubt that the key to our future lies in the past. With the end of the Mayan Calendar 12-21-2012 which holds unsurpassed calculations of cosmic cycles and time, we are left with many theories and possibilities.

Gregg is brilliant and if I were to condense his scientific offerings regarding 12-21-2012 it would take me until that date or longer to finish it, I then, wouldn't have time to publish all the information. I can tell you that if you're looking for a quick synopsis of scientific information regarding this event you may want to read his introduction in *The Mystery of 2012,* Choice Point 2012 filled with information regarding facts that we do know.

Scientists do know that the earth's magnetic field is decreasing and leaving a good possibility for reversal of the North and South poles which usually is preceded by abrupt changes in weather patterns. The sun is going through a magnetic shift, as well. An international team studying magnetoreception, the ability of human brains to detect magnetic changes in the earth, was discovered years ago. Our brains contain millions of tiny magnetic particles which connect all of us to the earth's magnetic field.

Correlations between magnetic fields of the Earth and the human experience suggest that it is easier for humans to adapt to change and new ideas within weaker magnetic fields.

In *The Divine Matrix* Gregg suggests that "We have all the power we need to create all the changes we choose". We're not just observers, we are the creators and we are all connected . . . he gives a formula to determine the number of people needed to work together to bring world peace and the figures are mind blowing! Only about 8,000 in a world of over 6 billion people

Through his research and calculations that if a certain percentage of human beings focus on the same outcome, at the same time, then we can co-create and make a global difference.

Think of it, perhaps if we combine Gregg's calculations with Barbara Marx Hubbard's Synergy Engine, an internet-based co-creative tool, bringing a new era of global coherence . . . then on "Day One" December 22, 2012, mankind may enter into a new state of divine consciousness

The Mother of Invention by Neale Donald Walsch, begins with an in depth look into the workings of life, inviting his readers to participate in reaching "what we are potentialed to be". He made up that word and it really works.

It was one of those OMG moments when I received my copy of his book in the mail! This shows connections and how coincidence happens for a reason. I had researched this upcoming date for several years and the day before the book arrived I had put the material aside deciding not to do this chapter because there was too much material, however I became inspired the more I read.

Here's the connections . . . I graduated from High School in Ashland, where the author lives and he is writing about a great lady who lives in Santa Barbara, which is where I lived just before my move to Las Vegas, where I had just finished reading Conversations with God book one, by Neale.

On the back inside cover of *Mother of Invention* is his picture taken by Christopher Briscoe, a well known photographer in southern Oregon who had taken my photo for business cards in Ashland. I had later helped Christopher at the Santa Barbara Airport . . . small world.

The Mother o f Invention, by Neale Donald Walsch, regarding the legacy of Barbara Marx Hubbard, one of modern day's greatest visionaries. Chapter 1 begins with "DAY ONE", December 22, 2012 . . . It is the day following the end of the world, coined by doomsayers . . . the setting is a huge stage in Phoenix, Arizona surrounded by Television Camera's, lights, boom mikes where Barbara waits to welcome crowds around the world to the new shift in humanity.

The Synergy Engine is a site where the entire world can participate, that is anyone with access to a computer can co-create with new optimistic views of what's needed and what works. We have smaller scale global community communications which are more ego based and don't work to the benefit of all since they weren't set up to benefit all humanity . . . we were still in the stages of "what's in it for me?" The heart didn't matter as much as the material.

If you choose to join Barbara in co-creating day one, December 22, 2012 you can. Information awaits you at <u>www.evolve.org</u>

See you there . . .

THE BEGINNING . . .

BIBLIOGRAPHY

I am deeply gratified and appreciate the knowledge and lessons that my Mentors continue bringing my way. They have provided me validation to my own experiences with their Education, Discoveries and great Works. I thank them all.

Baron-Reid, Colette www.colettebaronreid.com Messages from Spirit, Remembering the future

Braden, Gregg www.greggbraden.com Fractal Time, The Divine Matrix, Introduction: The mysteries of 2012 Choice Point; Introduction 2012

Browne, Sylvia www.sylviabrowne.com Phenomenon, Visits from the Afterlife

Dyer, Wayne W. www.drwaynedyer.com Manifest Your Destiny, Inspiration, The Power of Intention

Dovel, Matthew D. www.mylastbreath.com My Last Breath

Flaxman, Larry www.arpast.org 11:11 The time prompt phenomenon, Co-author, Marie D Jones

Hay, Louise L, www.LouiseHay.com You Can Heal Your Life www.Youcanhealyourlifemovie.com

Jones, Marie D. www.mariedjones.com 11:11 The time prompt phenomenon, Co-author Larry Flaxman

Kubler-Ross, Elisabeth www.EKRfoundation.org On Death And Dying, On Life after Death, The Wheel of Life, On Grief and Grieving Co-author David Kessler

Kessler, David www.grief.com Visions Trips and Crowded rooms, On Grief and Grieving

Mann, Ronald L www.ronmann.com Sacred Healing, Bouncing Back, Forward: Death & Divinity . . . how sweet it is

Marx Hubbard, Barbara www.evolve.com

Myss, Caroline www.myss.com Sacred Contracts

Rushnell, SQuire www.whengodwinks.com when God winks, when God winks on love

Smith, Gordon www.gordonsmithmedium.com Spirit Messenger

Varga, Josie www.josievarga.com Visits from heaven

Virtue, Doreen www.angeltherapy.com Messages from your Angels, Angel numbers 101

Walsch, Neale Donald www.Nealedonaldwalsch.com The Mother of Invention, Conversations with God

Weiss, Brian L. www.brianweiss.com Many Lives, Many Masters, Only Love is Real, Mirrors of Time

Wilde, Stuart www.stuartwilde.com Sixth Sense, The Trick to Money Is Having Some

Wyland, www.wyland.com The Art of Wyland

Acknowledgements

Thank you is not enough to my best friend Barbara, because you lost your life when we were sixteen, it put me on my journey. I knew that you had died before I was told . . . which I did not understand! Because of you I began to question what life is all about . . . I hope you like some of the answers I came up with . . .

Bon Bon . . . my beautiful friend of ten years, who died after a brave battle with cancer. Thank You for hanging in there while I raced to the hospital to say goodbye and I Love you.

Thanks to my Auntie V. who Loved so many . . . I wish you could be here for my book, but I know that you'll be reading it there . . . you have been an inspiration to us all.

Thank you my cousins for being . . . and being there for me . . . my awesome Cousins Linda and Peter, Brad, and my two gorgeous 2nd cousins Katherine and Elisabeth. My Cousins Jim and Rich and your wonderful wives, children and grandchildren.

A very Special Thanks to all of you who have allowed me to include your story. Know that each of you have touched me deeply, and that others are sure to be touched, as well.

Bonny J, my best friend in Grants Pass; who I've known since the fifth grade. Thanks for your uplifting spirit. You bring much humor to me.

Ricky, my best friend in Santa Barbara . . . Thanking you for your uplifting spirits and perception on life . . . and men.

Darlene, my best friend on Maui, you've always been an inspiration, your crazy humor . . . Thanks for being you.

Bobby, my best neighbor ever! We've shared a million laughs and mentally written that many books. Thank you for always believing in my work.

Billie, my best friend in Waco, thanks for adding many healthy laughs to my life.

Stevee, my best friend somewhere on some golf course . . . I've always appreciated your thoughts and perceptions on life, a little crazy, a little far-out, but you are most creative and a fabulous photographer.

Linda, Thanks and keep smiling I appreciate your support and understanding while I'm writing.

Thanks to all of you, whom I may have missed, but didn't mean to . . .

Last but not least, my heartfelt Thanks to Auntie Sandee , my dear friend and my son's nurse who I've known since the mid 70's in Honolulu. You were always there for me through the good times and the not so good times. You inspired me as my world was crashing down and I shall never forget your kindness. The least I could do, which I did, was introduce you to the man of your dreams . . . your marvelous husband, Dick.

AFTERWORD

One most amazing man alive on our planet is Dannion Brinkley who has experienced three NDE's, well documented, Near Death Experiences. *Saved By The LIGHT* is his true account of having died twice and then after that book was published he encountered a third NDE, however it was his first Near Death Experience which brought this term into the mainstream consciousness.

His books are sure to blow the mind of many *Skeptics* and perhaps they will question their own logic and find the illusion. Dannion was a skeptic and very pragmatic, until the mid seventies when lightning struck, immediately electrocuting him, at which time he left his body and was viewing himself and everything from above. Until that time he did not believe in Angels or the hereafter, but he found himself traveling down a tunnel of light to a place unlike he'd ever seen before. His visit there changed his life forever, including extreme psychic abilities.

As a result of his experiences he lost all fear of death, as I have lost my fear. The Heavens brought him much insight to truths, just as I was given a glimpse of the Cosmic in my OBE, Out Of Body Experience. Dannion devotes a great deal of time working with Hospice. You can catch his account of events, and more about his books at his website: www.dannion.com. He has co-founded "The Twilight Brigade" which is dedicated to end of life care at the bedside of the dying, especially our nation's veterans, focused at VA Hospitals across the country. Because he's visited "the other side" he brings peace, hope and inspiration to the terminally ill, their friends and family.

Much is being said today of "Earth Angels", who serve as cosmic intermediaries and messengers whom bring us communications from higher realms. I believe Dannion to be one of those Angels because of the work he has done with the dying and also by his predictions.

As I was finishing up Death and Divinity an important thought crossed my mind…what was really the goal for my book? It dawned on me that if I could help just one human being loose their fear of death then my life experiences will all have been for the good…

I found myself being forced to move from a place I loved but as it turned out I moved, not far away where I met a new neighbor, a lovely ninety-four year old lady. She is an inspiration to the entire community and her zest for life is unmatched. Because of Anita Elliott, I now have attained my goal. It was the evening she said, and this was before having read my book, "Judy, I think that we have met, so that you could help me loose my fear of Death".

I have become inspired to move in the direction of Hospice, and am presently involved with certification courses on-line.